MOUNTAINS TO CLIMB

A HANDBOOK OF RESOURCES FOR THE GIFTED AND TALENTED

by

Patricia A. Haensly

William R. Nash

Published by
National Association for Gifted Children
5100 N. Edgewood Dr. • St. Paul, MN 55112

This informational document was supported by a grant from
the College of Education, Texas A&M University.

Contents

Acknowledgments

No manuscript is complete without an expression of appreciation to people who have contributed to it in special ways, above and beyond the writing of the material. One of those special people has been Dr. William R. Nash—his vision for creative projects, quiet persistent support of those who undertake such projects and his dedication to serving gifted youth are exemplary. These qualities have assisted others to accomplish things they would not have otherwise done. It has been my good fortune to collaborate with him on this particular project which was meant to serve gifted youth in a special way.

A group of people who have provided a special kind of inspiration are the children of the authors, the students with whom we have worked, and especially the students of the Career Experience Opportunity 1980-81 Program for gifted and talented high school seniors of A&M Consolidated High School in College Station, Texas. Valuable editorial comments and suggestions about the content of the guide were given by Peter Ray. The cover was designed by Blyth Hazen. Both Peter and Blyth were students in the above program. Their insightful comments, as well as those of the other students in the program, have contributed much to the ideas expressed in the guide.

In addition, many suggestions and ideas were contributed through personal conversations with individuals who have taught, parented, or otherwise worked with gifted students. We are especially grateful to them and to my fellow graduate students in the gifted education program at Texas A&M for their generosity in sharing ideas about appropriate provisions for the gifted.

Finally, one of the most important contributors to any manuscript is the individual who wades through pages of material, extracting sense and order out of strange instructions, in order to type the material and bring it into communicable existence. We are very grateful for the good humor, patience and expertise of Peggy Locke who undertook this latter task!

Patricia Haensly

Preface

The intent of this resource guide has been to offer suggestions, directed to you as gifted and talented youth, regarding the types of experiences that can provide the educational enrichment and acceleration which are vital to your intellectual and creative development. These suggestions are meant to add to the provisions that should be made by the schools, public or private; or, in some cases, to inform you so that you can make better use of resources which are already centered in the schools. Since local school districts do not always meet the needs of the gifted in their mainstream of education, we believe that YOU *can and must* take the initiative through creative planning and persistence to overcome this handicap. We hope that this guide will provide relevant information about where to locate and how to take advantage of the opportunities which are most suited to your particular gifts and talents.

CHAPTER ONE

Mountains to Climb

So–you believe that you're G I F T E D or, in better terms, perhaps, 'brighter or more talented than the average individual'. What can Y O U do to develop those 'gifts', and to use those talents in a way that is satisfying to you?

What can you do to really put that mind of yours to work, to put it into high gear? What can you do to exercise those little used skills you have? And how can you explore those fascinating unknowns and sample new cerebral adventures? You're ready to climb the mental Himalayas and all you've been doing is running in the foothills, or worse yet, running on a treadmill.

Your school has a great alternative program for people interested in academics–literature, history, journalism, and the like; you're in a challenging physics class, and your math instructor has individualized his calculus class so that you're working way ahead of your classmates. OR, your school *doesn't* have any of these things. But, either way, you're looking for something beyond the school curriculum that will challenge you, some ways in which you can take control of your mind's work in your own most individual style. The mountains are there to climb but YOU want to PLAN THE EXPEDITIONS! How do you make BASE CAMP?

That's what this resource guide is all about. Some of it has to do with the MOUNTAINS there are to climb, much of it has to do with where to establish the BASE CAMPS, and how and where to train for each mountain's challenge and obstacles. Read on then for a complete itinerary, or pick and choose the chapters that seem the most relevant to your needs.

CHAPTER TWO

But Wait! To Accelerate or to Enrich?

To hurry on ahead OR to examine all the nooks and crannies–that is the question–whether it is better in the long run to reach quickly for the peak of one's own special mountain or to explore the many mountains that might be climbed. Both are ways of soaring and both have their satisfactions and limitations. Actually, neither should be at the expense of eliminating the other. But, *you* have the right to decide which is best for *you!*

Skipping grades is probably the first and simplest thing that comes to mind as a way of moving ahead more quickly. For those of you who have achieved well in most of your courses, with scores consistently at the 97th to 99th percentile on your school's regularly administered standardized achievement-test batteries (such as the Iowa Test of Basic Skills, the California, Stanford, or Metropolitan Achievement Test), or have done well on specially administered tests such as the SAT, you or your parents may have little difficulty in convincing the school to permit you to bypass grades. The best time to do this is at the end of elementary, middle, or junior high school, skipping the last grade of one of these divisions. This overcomes problems of social outlets and acceptance by classmates; others will also be making new friends, so you will not be conspicuously different.

A LIMITATION to this solution of broad grade skipping is that some of you who have exceptionally high ability in science or math and may be ready for twelfth-grade calculus, may only be ready for ninth-grade English or social studies, or vice versa. You also will need to allow for state requirements such as health education, and sequence courses such as Algebra I and II, managing these courses through correspondence courses, tutoring or doing outside work for that subject. You may also just not want to miss some opportunity of a particular grade or school.

Twelve-year-old Sorajini, who was ready for 9th grade math, insisted that her parents not tell the teachers that she had already covered the 7th grade language arts reading material, *because* she didn't want to miss the chance to participate in the debate emphasis that she knew would be available in that language arts course. She had determined that she could accept the reading material for a year, especially since she had been enrolled in the 9th grade Algebra as a special arrangement. And after a two-week National Science Foundation summer session at a nearby college, she had a lot of ideas to follow through in her year's science course, as well as some peer and teacher friendships from there to keep her in touch.[1]

A special class arrangement option, then, may often be a better solution if you (and your parents) can arrange with your school to have you placed in an advanced math class, or history class, or language arts, while still carrying on with your agemates in other courses.

If you can latch on to **a mentor,** or very interested tutor, you will have found an excellent solution to establishing the perfect accelerated pace for you combined with the stimulation of working with another enthusiast in your area of interest. Mentors may be found in many places—nearby universities, small colleges, libraries, museums, successful businesses; professional women and men are often very receptive to bright and interested youth. People who are fluent in another language, some of whom have more time to share because of age or limited jobs, may be very willing to help you improve your communication in that language—and perhaps share some cultural background with you. Sometimes, you can approach the prospective mentor to ask if he or she would share some of their expertise with you; sometimes, a parent's or teacher's request will set the stage for these special type relationships. If you're well-read and enthusiastic about your subject, eager to learn from the expert, and willing to adjust your schedule to their available time, few professionals will be able to resist at least a meeting or two. If your enthusiasms match, you may have found yourself a mentor-relationship. If not, you may be referred to someone else or you may have to search again; in any case, an appropriate thank you will assure your continued welcome for later questions or references.

---

[1]Personal communication.

Charles Fefferman, at 30, one of the brilliant mathematicians of this century, recently won the Waterman award, an award which provided him with a $150,000 fellowship and time to spend just thinking about problems in modern mathematical analysis. As a sixth grader, however, Charlie's parents asked a math professor at the University of Maryland to talk with their son about his consuming interest in math. Every week that summer, Charlie and Professor Hummel met once a week for mathematical talk; by the next summer it was obvious that Charlie was destined to become a mathematician, and by the time he was 14 he was enrolled at Maryland fulltime. Professor Hummel had been the mentor who had guided Charlie's math thinking for awhile and then helped make arrangements so that Charlie could move on ahead.[2]

E, a successful administrative assistant to the president of a well-known university, recalled that one of her first and most helpful mentors was the librarian in the small town where she grew up. They shared discussions of books, the librarian guided E's search for the best in literature, and laid the groundwork for E's later excellence in that field. What started out as an enriching experience for E, stimulated her love for reading and became an accelerating force for a career in writing and literature.[3]

College courses under special release time are an option for junior high and high school students with advanced mathematics and science or literature skills. The work in college courses is usually quite *fast-paced,* which may offer you much intellectual stimulation. College courses usually spend about one-fourth as many classroom hours on the same material as would be covered in a high school class. You will need to be able to *work independently and rapidly* between classes, but you will usually be able to enlist the help of the college instructor with difficult problems. And you will have to *be your own*

---

[2]Bode, Carl. One of the great mathematicians of the 20th Century. *ITYB (Intellectually Talented Youth Bulletin),* 1979, 5(10), 18-19.
[3]Personal communication.

pacemaker for getting in homework assignments and studying for exams. If these are characteristics that fit your learning style, then a local university or college will be one of your best assets. Your achievement test records, recommendation from your guidance counselor, if your school has one, and recommendations from your principal are the usual necessary keys to admission, along with a diplomatic (nonofficious) persistence at contacting and meeting with the officials who will help you to make these arrangements. Junior or community colleges may also fill the bill for this type of acceleration, but you should examine their course offerings and perhaps talk to their instructors to insure that the pace and content of the courses will challenge you and actually move you forward.

The DISADVANTAGES for the college class option include the special *arrangements and transportation* that may be involved, *scheduling* with the rest of the school's program, and *possible costs* (which will depend on the college and your school district).

The ADVANTAGES are the *intellectual stimulation* and *challenge* that will have its spillover effect on all of the other things you do, the *faster 'moving on'* to the exciting things you'd like to do with your mind and life, and, perhaps most importantly, the opportunity to *associate intellectually* at a level more appropriate for you. Taking college courses, while still enrolled in junior or senior high school, can also be one of the most economical ways of advancing one's total educational program.

Many students are already taking advantage of **graduation in three years** from high school. This may require doubling up on English courses, or a summer course, but is possible with careful planning for most capable youth. You will have to plan your course schedule early to accommodate sequence or series courses where more than one semester's offering must be taken to obtain credit, and in order to satisfy state or district requirements. Skipping the senior, or even junior year of high school is a possibility, but it must be planned with the requirements in mind for the college of your choice; not all colleges look with favor on early admission. Some high schools may grant a diploma after successful completion of one year of college, if having this accreditation is a concern.

This kind of acceleration and very **early admission to college** are special trademarks of Stanley's program.[4] If the mathematical or physical sciences (and computer sciences), and entrance to Johns Hopkins more than a year early are of special interest to you, you might consider writing to Professor Stanley, telling him about yourself and your progress and scores in math, and ask him about his program at Johns Hopkins: Professor Julian C. Stanley, Study of Mathematically Precocious Youth (SMPY), Department of Psychology, THE JOHNS HOPKINS UNIVERSITY, Baltimore, Maryland 21218. (Or, ask about the program for verbally precocious youth.)

If the options just described don't sound like possibilities in your case, or are not the route you'd like to take, then you may want to consider the alternative of EXPLORATION or ENRICHMENT. Exploring may be a necessary step for you at this moment in time, and may be more necessary in the understanding of your role in a society of achievement and productivity than hurrying on ahead.

The **honors courses** which some high schools and most colleges offer are a possibility for such exploration. The content of these courses is covered in greater depth and breadth than in the regular class. The ADVANTAGES of these courses include the *small, stimulating classes, outstanding instructors, close faculty-student ties,* and the *recognition on your academic record* (sometimes helpful in gaining admission to special schools or advanced scholarship awards). The Texas A&M University brochure states that "Students in an Honors section should expect to work slightly harder than in a non-honors one, but without undue worry about grades."

Some schools have an Honors Studies Curriculum which requires specific courses for graduation with that recognition. Pan American University at Edinburgh requires 3 specific courses, which includes a two-part Western civilization course in the freshman year to give students a broad overview of intellectual heritage and relate knowledge gleaned from other courses and studies. Admission to Pan American's program is extended to entering freshmen who graduated in the top quarter of their high school class with a combined SAT score of 1100 or above, or if graduating in the second or lower quarters

[4]Stanley, J.C. Enter Johns Hopkins early? *ITYB,* 1979, 5(10), 29-30.

of their high school class, with a SAT minimum of 1200. Write to the University Honors Program or the Director of Honors Studies of the college you plan to attend for information specific for that college.

Some colleges also offer such things as a **January term**, which utilizes a month between fall and spring semesters to offer specially tailored experiences such as uninterrupted work in a biology lab or out in the field, production of a complete magazine issue, intensive instrumental music lessons, or a period of time teaching in a special setting.

At the college level, **study abroad** is becoming a frequent offering of many colleges and universities. These programs require you to provide sufficient funds to cover travel as well as tuition and living expenses. The opportunity is especially suited to foreign language studies, political science or historical searches, art, and music specialties, and to the study of the literature and culture of foreign countries. At the high school level, exchange programs with other countries provide similar cultural exploration for a semester or longer. Language study programs often sponsor shorter summer experiences, such as trips to Mexico. Church youth groups sometimes participate in cooperative work programs with isolated cultures within the United States, such as Appalachia, or in adjoining countries.

While the college course options enrich your knowledge base as well as moving you ahead, you may prefer to broaden your knowledge base in a less restrictive environment, one where YOU determine how deeply you will pursue a topic and what creative measures you will take, and where your pursuit will not be limited by class or semester time-frames and examination objectives. Perhaps you'd like to take time to develop your own special contribution—an intergalactic space traveler, or a novel, or a jazz concerto for saxophone. Even though you're in a world guided heavily by achievement and productivity, you may feel the need to learn in a less goal-oriented atmosphere about the intricacies of diatoms or solar systems, about the War of the Roses or King Arthur and Medieval History, about the poetry of Carl Sandburg or science fiction, or the real needs of Appalachian families. As the psalmist might put it:

> "a time to move ahead quickly,
> and a time to reflect and ponder and grow."

This kind of enrichment can be obtained in experiences which range from **drama clubs to summer science camps, youth organizations to work experiences, private lessons to historical societies.** The opportunities for these experiences are suggested in more detail in Chapters 4 through 9. Or, you may prefer and be able to proceed more independently, designing your own format for intellectual growth. In **designing your own format,** as in the planned experiences mentioned above, finding individuals who can and will share their expertise with you, and the creative stimulation of working with others who have a similar interest and objective are important elements to keep in mind.

Before we leave the subject of deciding between acceleration and enrichment, a few words about making the choice are appropriate. A study of young students between the ages of 15 and 18 who came to Johns Hopkins University during 1976 and 1977 was reported in a book by Ann Eisenberg and William George, "College and University" Winter, 1979 (American Association of Collegiate Registrars and Admissions Officers, One Dupont Circle, Washington, 20036; single copy $3). The authors state that students who enter college early, even by as much as three years, perform as well academically, or better, than their classmates, and do not seem to be socially or emotionally handicapped. Girls and boys both solve their dating problems well, and even proms when important can be managed.

For some students, time spent in boring, unchallenging courses when they could be moving ahead more quickly and deeply, becomes a very oppressive and deteriorating situation, a feeling of wasting away. Being challenged and at ease with what you are doing intellectually or academically can keep the personal problems in their proper perspective. Problems (which may accompany moving out of your age group) such as developing interpersonal skills and a positive self-concept, resolving your own identity, and learning to work and play with others are all ones which must be dealt with by both gifted and average people with agemates or across ages. Not all adults understand the additional discouragement of highly able youth who want fervently to challenge their minds and test the limits of their capabilities, even though such determined desire is much akin to the spirit that made pioneers cross deserts and mountains to settle new lands, and makes athletes strive to break Olympic records! Don't hesitate to seek out your school counselor to talk about your problems and feelings, or a trusted teacher who understands the needs of gifted individuals.

Many bright students are able to manage the accelerative activities already described and still find time to enjoy participating in band, sports, cheerleading, student government, music lessons, debate or other extracurricular activities. Students such as Charlie Fefferman, described previously, were fortunate to have families who helped them see the need for recreational time with agemates. During his early years at University of Maryland, Charlie was known back home as "a kid with a nice sense of humor" and he regularly spent time after school with these friends. Social development, then, is a problem which you, with your family's help, must attend to wisely.

For some students who skip grades and then are in courses that are no more interesting or challenging, acceleration can be an unhappy solution. For very creative individuals, instructional mediocrity in the new grade will not improve an education that has not stimulated creative problem solving in previous grades and the press of more dull work may quickly stifle any enthusiasm for school or learning.

You may have to do battle with red tape, and you may have to be very persistent and persuasive to tailor your education to your needs, to find the right level of challenge and accomplishment for you. If you can search out teachers for whom you are able to put forth your best efforts, you will find yourself with tremendous advocates. Even in the smallest high schools, you should be able to find a teacher who will go to bat for a really special student, who will help you find resources to develop your special abilities. Battling the red tape may require your most skillful diplomacy, rather than an aggressive stance. Don't be afraid to ask questions, and to search for the best options for yourself (there are many listed above and in the next chapter). Also, don't be undone by not knowing WHAT YOU WANT TO DO IN LIFE! You may need to use the options which allow you the breadth for exploration.

Do *savour* the good opportunities that come along. Richard Cohn, a math accelerant from Johns Hopkins,[5] says in the

---

[5]Cohn, R.J. Thoughts on acceleration. *ITYB*, 1979, 5(10),7.

Summer-1979 *Intellectually Talented Youth Bulletin,* that he remembers the special enjoyment of taking college courses as a junior and senior high student. The challenge and interest of working with intellectual peers put those classes into a category not always matched by later courses taken while actually in college. Too, there often may be outstanding teachers in your high school advanced electives, whose quality of teaching will not be matched later. "Advanced electives" seems to be the key–teachers here are able to make the magic of *learning with enjoyment* happen. And an opportunity to spend a year as a high school exchange student in Germany may have to be balanced against early entry into college. The tradeoff value will depend on what your goals are. It may be helpful to list the costs and returns (personal, financial, academic) on some kind of ledger. Then choose the course that will provide you with the most personal satisfaction, both long and short range.

While the next section has to do specifically with acceleration, most of this resource guide will have to do with the kind of enrichment that broadens your experience base as you move forward. But whichever you do, SET YOUR SIGHTS FOR SOARING.

CHAPTER THREE

The Options for Acceleration into and Through College

"The simplest way to finish college young is to start early" says Frank Laycock, a professor at Oberlin College, and author of the book *Gifted Children.*[6] In fact, years ago, Robert Hutchins (you may recognize him as the originator of the Great Books Program) started a plan for accepting bright high school sophomores and juniors at the University of Chicago where they could proceed at their own speed by passing achievement tests whenever they felt ready. And in California, bright students who pass a test for a high school diploma (originally intended for dropouts) can enter a university without their senior year of high school. But why would you want to get into the March Hare and Mad Hatter's act, "We're late, we're late, for a very important date"? Two main reasons:

1. So you can get to where you're going sooner, and do significant things in an area of fascination earlier and longer in your life time.

James Watson had his Ph.D. degree at age twenty-three and had earned a Nobel prize for his DNA model before twenty-five.

Michaelangelo was still active as an architect of St. Peter's from the age 72 until his death at 89, but his works of art spanned a life's work begun in his youth–by 17 he had completed such famous works as "Battle of the Centaurs" and "The Faun".

2. So you can become an expert in one interest area and still have time to achieve excellence in another–either for your leisure or for your productive work (though both may overlap)!

Gauguin was a prosperous stockbroker before he switched to a career in art at 35.

Merrill Kenneth Wolf, who now is a prominent neuroanatomist and talented musician graduated from Yale University shortly after his fourteenth birthday, having studied piano under Paul Hindemuth.

---

[6]Laycock, F. *Gifted Children.* Glenview, IL: Scott, Foresman & Co., 1979.

Rachel Carson, who published her first story at age 10, was inspired by a brilliant biology teacher in her junior year of college, went on to do graduate work in genetics at Johns Hopkins University, became one of the first two women to be hired by the U.S. Bureau of Fisheries in Washington, and became an avid advocate for conservation of the sea *(The Sea Around Us)* and birds *(Silent Spring)*. A New York Times reviewer said "rarely does the world get a physical scientist with literary genius."

As life spans increase, the option of several lifetime careers becomes more and more realistic.

Edith Clarke, who became a teacher of math and physics after a Vassar College degree, decided to study civil engineering at the University of Wisconsin; she became a "computer" for American Telephone and Telegraph, received the first Master of Science degree granted to a woman at MIT, and later patented an invention to predict behavior of a system without complicated equation-solving. Returning to college teaching, she wrote a graduate text on circuit analysis which is still a standard.

Frank B. Ryan was a professional football star (as quarterback he led the Cleveland Browns to World Championship in 1964), received his Ph.D. in math from Rice in 1965, and is now the director of the House Information Systems Committee in the U.S. House of Representatives.

Now then, how do you accomplish this exceptionally early start? If the route is an academic one, that is, university level study is the reasonable avenue to your career, then the following options should be considered.

ENTERING COLLEGE WITH ADVANCED STANDING

A paperback book, authored by Gene R. Hawes and recently published by McGraw-Hill, "Getting College Course Credits by Examination to Save $$$", has directions assembled for the many ways to enter college with credits already accumulated towards a degree (or even how to complete a degree). In addition, the book contains a listing of 2100 colleges and universities and the exam series that they recognize, gives suggestions on how to study for specific exams, and most helpfully, takes you step by step through the major options. It contains a wealth of utilitarian information on AP, CLEP, PEP–on credit by exam!

It should be pointed out that not all educators agree that obtaining college credits by passing examinations is an equal substitute to advanced study under master teachers, with peer interaction. If you can bypass a required course that would offer little challenge because you're overqualified, or obtain a degree necessary for further work in the field without expending $$ which you can't manage, then your decision is simplified. Especially if the $$ saved buys you the option to go on to a professional school–law, medicine, etc. OR buys you time to broaden your intellectual scope!

(Special Note: Although the examples provided with the options described in this chapter are derived from only a few colleges in Texas, it must be kept in mind that you, as a prospective student, will need to explore the policies of the college of your choice, either in other localities in Texas, or in other regions of the country. These examples merely illustrate the variety of policies held by different schools.)

These are the routes that you can take for advanced standing:

ADVANCED PLACEMENT PROGRAM (APP)

1. *WHAT* is APP? This program sponsors college level courses, ordinarily undertaken in high school, taught or directed by designated AP teachers, which can be translated into college credit by performing at an acceptable level on APP-designed exams, exams which are given once a year at APP participating high schools.

2. *INFORMATION:* If your school has the APP, see your school's AP coordinator. If not, write for the name and address of an AP coordinator at a nearby high school:

AP Exams
Box 977-IS
Princeton, NJ 08540

Or, phone (609) 921-9000 and ask for Institutional Services. You can also obtain bulletin copies and general information from:

AP Program
College Entrance Examination Board
888 Seventh Ave.
New York, NY 10019
(212) 582-6210

Or, write for free Item No. 273654 "Some Questions and Answers about the Advanced Placement Program" from:

College Board Publication Orders
Box 2815
Princeton, NJ 08541

Full and current official information on each recommended AP course and exam is given in an "Advanced Placement Course Description" booklet for each of the 14 subjects (24 exams) offered in the program and may be obtained for a nominal fee.

3. *WHO* can take AP courses? Seniors, juniors, even sophomores can take the courses, although you may have to fight your way into them (that is, give evidence to school administrators of strong determination to see the course through). Plan ahead in the ninth or tenth grade so that you will have the appropriate background courses to take the AP courses in your junior or senior year. Just be sure to take the exams in the same year that you take the course or do your own independent studying. Since these are college level learning experiences they may take more studying in depth, but they can offer you more stimulation and greater opportunities for accomplishment.

4. *WHICH* courses to take? Decide on which to try for depending on your strongest areas *and* the college to which you will apply. College catalogs will sometimes list the ones for which they will offer credit (Pan American University has an extensive listing), or you may need to write to the Director of Admissions for the college(s) of your choice. Most of the nation's colleges give credit for individually specified AP exam grades, including Harvard, Stanford, and Vassar.

Texas A&M University awards up to a full year of credit for a score of 3 or higher on the appropriate AP exams in 5 of the subject areas (American History, Calculus, Chemistry, English or Physics) and 3 credit hours for a score of 4 on the Biology exam.

If your high school doesn't offer AP, you may be able to study with the help of interested teachers and the books and literature suggested by APP.

5. *WHY* do it? A full year's credits via AP could be worth over $8000 in college costs for the price of $32 for each examination (with a limited number of fee reductions to $15 for students with financial need). This $ saving in college costs may make the difference for you of even obtaining a college degree. Or, this $ saving may allow you the option of going to a more prestigious institution, or one with a specific concentration in your field of interest, rather than a less desirable, cheaper college. Many students are able to start college as sophomores by doing well on AP exams, thus saving the cost of a whole year of college.

6. *WHEN & WHERE* are the exams given? APP exams are given the 3rd week in May *only,* during an approximately 3-hour testing time for each exam, at APP participating high schools.

7. *SCORES* are sent to the student's home address, school, and college if requested. Exams combine multiple choice questions and essay questions and are graded on the 5-point scale by a group of college and high school teachers assembled by the program. (A grade of 5 signifies extremely qualified, 3 qualified, and 1 no recommendation.)

COLLEGE-LEVEL EXAMINATION PROGRAM (CLEP)

1. *WHAT?* CLEP is a national program for obtaining college credit by examination, sponsored by the College Entrance Examination Board (CEEB) (who also administer the SAT exam and the AP Program); CLEP is designed to recognize with college credit, achievement or advanced learning gained through personal reading, on-the-job ex-

perience, or independent study.

2. *INFORMATION* may be obtained from:

> College Level Examination Program
> The College Board
> 888 Seventh Ave.
> New York, NY 10019
> (212) 582-6210

or from the CLEP office at ETS which administers CLEP exams:

> CLEP, The College Board
> Box 1822
> Princeton, NJ 08540
> (609) 921-9000

Ask for "CLEP General and Subject Examinations, Descriptions, and Sample Questions".

3. *WHO?* Anyone who believes that they are already qualified to omit material covered during college courses. If you have been well read in any of the subject areas and have done any independent study of the material, CLEP exams may be well worth your time.

4. WHICH? CLEP General Examinations are designed to measure familiarity with material covered in different subject areas during the first two years of college in order to meet the general education or liberal arts requirement. The 5 subject areas are English Composition, Humanities, Mathematics, Natural Sciences, and Social Sciences and History. Not all colleges accept CLEP General Examination scores for credit (Texas A&M University does not). Other schools, such as Southwestern University, accept CLEP General Examination scores under specified directions; (e.g., 3 semester credit hours toward a degree may be awarded for a score of 52 or better in any of the subject areas, but can only be used as elective credits). CLEP Subject Examinations are designed to assess knowledge gained from specific college courses, and as such are again accepted with specific limitations set by each college or university, according to their determination as to how nearly the exam matches their own course offering objectives. The Subject Examinations are offered in 8 dif-

ferent areas, including foreign languages, nursing and medical technology.

Texas A&M University lists 16 CLEP Subject Examinations that they will accept; for example, American Literature, General Chemistry, and Money and Banking, with minimum scores of 52, 50, and 45 required, respectively. A score of 65 on the General Chemistry exam gives you credit for an additional advanced chemistry series. And on the American Literature, you must qualify on both the Objective and Essay parts of the CLEP exam.

Since each college has its own specific requirements about tests they will accept for credit and the amount of credit given, it is best to consult the catalogs or Director of Admissions or Counseling and Testing Office for each and any of the schools in which you are interested, making your decision based upon the school you plan to enter.

5. *WHY?* For the same reason as given above for the AP Program, and especially when APP hasn't been available to you. The cost can range from $22 for one test taken at a specified test center at specified times to $76 for four tests, plus $25 when special arrangements are made for a more convenient location of the test administration.

6. *WHEN & WHERE* are the exams given? The 90-minute CLEP tests are given during a one-week period of each month (with the exception that none are administered in December or February) at colleges and universities which are listed in "Moving Ahead with CLEP" (ordered from addresses given under Information, above).

7. *SCORES:* Scores are sent to you or a specified college within about 4 weeks after you've taken the test. The exams are multiple choice type, but an optional essay form is available which should be taken only if required by the college you plan to attend, and it is graded by the college from which you seek college credit. (The multiple choice questions and the essay portion of the General Examination in English Composition with Essay is graded by the College Board.)

PROFICIENCY EXAMINATION PROGRAM (PEP)

1. *WHAT?* PEP is another national program for obtaining college credit by exam, but is sponsored by the American College Testing Program (who administers the ACT exam).

2. *INFORMATION* and forms may be obtained from:

>ACT Proficiency Examination Program
>American College Testing Program
>Box 168
>Iowa City, IA 52240
>(319) 356-3711

You may also request the "PEP List of Participating Institutions" and the free "PEP Candidate Registration Guide." Or ask for the free ACT PEP Study Guide for each examination from:

>ACT PEP Study Guides
>Box 168
>Iowa City, IA 52240

3. *WHO?* Anyone who will be seeking credit at a college or university that requires the ACT entrance exam *and* specifies PEP as the credit-by-examination route. But be sure to check with your college to see if they accept PEP.

4. *WHICH?* Any of their approximately 45 different subject exams. If you are especially interested in business administration and nursing, PEP may be a good route to take; PEP also offers unusual exams in law enforcement.

5. *WHY?* As with CLEP and APP. The fee for taking most of the individual exams is $25-$35.

6. *WHEN & WHERE?* The first Thursday and Friday of February, May, August and November at specified test centers; you must register 5 or 6 weeks before a test date.

7. *SCORES:* No report of scores is sent to a college unless you request it; you can wait and decide after you've received the report. The 3-hour exams vary in type between objective (multiple choice and true/false) and essay, with no penalty for guessing on the items. Typically 3-6 semester hour credits are given for acceptable performance.

DEPARTMENTAL EXAMINATIONS

1. *WHAT?* Colleges and universities frequently offer their own program for granting credit by exam. Such programs are usually integrated with their school's acceptance of particular exams from one of the above listed programs (APP, CLEP, PEP), and credit hours may be awarded with or without a grade.

> Pan American University (Edinburgh, TX) offers college credit-by-exam for qualified students with APP (such as 8 credit hours in Chemistry for a score of 4 or 5), ACT subsections (3 credit hours of freshman English with a score of 26 or 27 on the English section of ACT, 6 credit hours with 28) and CLEP. A detailed list of credits allowed for different courses, along with the grades given for specific scores, is given in the catalog. Advanced standing exams must be cleared with department heads.

> Texas Women's University (Denton, TX) offers credit by exam by APP, CLEP, Departmental Exams, and Professional Society Tests in Specific Disciplines.

> Texas A&M University offers credit by exam for 9 specified AP exams, 16 specified CLEP Subject Exams (*no* CLEP General Exams), and Departmental Exams which may be taken only with specified minimum scores on SAT or CEEB Achievement Tests (although no specifications are given for modern languages Departmental Exams).

As you can see, no two schools will have the same specifications and many of the procedures will not be found in written policy. *Your* best policy then is to pursue your individual case as diplomatically and persistently as you can through channels such as Academic Counseling and Testing Centers, Director of Admissions, or even directly with departments in which you seek to major. Most schools will work carefully with incoming students (especially highly qualified ones) to assure the best fit between credits allowed and courses to be taken. Early pursuit (rather than late registration week) is suggested.

2. *INFORMATION* may be obtained by consulting with or writing to the Director of Admissions or the Academic Counseling Center of the school of your choice. The most efficient way to proceed is to plan ahead with the school you plan to enter so that you can take these exams along with any summer or fall orientation program the school may offer, and so that you can integrate AP or CLEP exams with the departmental ones you want to take.

3. *WHO?* Any "qualified" student. The key word is "qualified", and the particulars are spelled out by each college or university.

> At Texas A&M University, you must have scored 600 or more on the Verbal part of the SAT to take the departmental test in biology. By contrast, a student who scores 650 or more on the CEEB English Composition Achievement Test will receive credit for English 103 and the option to take the department exam for English 104, but, if scoring 600-649, will receive credit for English 103 and is not eligible to take the departmental exam for English 104.

4. *WHICH?* So then, your decisions about which to take must be based on your areas of strength, along with the requirements of the school you plan to attend. It would also be a good idea to check with special departments within the school, since departments too have their own requirements and policies.

5. *WHY?* As before, to "get ahead faster" and to get into more challenging and interesting courses, or into the courses best suited for the *level* of your knowledge.

6. *WHEN & WHERE?* They are given at the school you plan to attend, usually during freshman orientation. Usually no fee is involved; for example, at Texas A&M, no fee is charged if given before the first day of classes in your initial semester.

7. *SCORES:* Since each department sets its own require-

ment, you need to check with each one in which you are interested. It would be wise to plan carefully if you're concerned about grade point averages and later entry into highly competitive professional programs. For example, coming up with the minimum acceptance score for credit in a course that is highly important to your field, might be the basis for declining the credit, taking the course, and doing well in it. For a course that is only a peripheral requirement to that professional field, you might consider accepting the credit and moving on to other offerings. *DO* weigh the pros and cons.

HIGH SCHOOL/COLLEGE CONCURRENT ENROLLMENT

COURSES IN COLLEGE CURRICULA

Some universities have initiated a program in which high school students can enroll in university courses as part of their high school program. Advantages of this procedure are that you can enjoy the high school atmosphere and activities and still have the challenging experience of being in the university setting. You're usually accepted as just another student by faculty and students, although sometimes held in awe when other students find out that you're "only a high school student"–it's your choice whether to let this be known. Also, you can get the feel for college level demands and the knowledge of college facilities and customs without the pressures of being limited entirely to this setting. The courses are taken on a released time or night basis and must be fitted into the remainder of your high school schedule, so you may have scheduling and transportation problems to work out. Another advantage is the cost, since college credit for the courses may sometimes be allowed upon college entry, even though you took the course for high school credit.

Texas A&M University offers the High School Enrichment Program (HSEP) for superior students from the three local high schools. HSEP is administered by the TAMU University Honors

Program Office, whose director is Dr. B. L. Shapiro.

Angelina College (Lufkin, TX) and West Texas State University (Canyon, TX) offer admission on an individual basis for superior students who have completed their junior year of high school; they state that their purpose is to provide academic challenge, not to replace or abbreviate the high school program. Graduation from high school is the prerequisite for release of the credits earned through an official transcript. (This stipulation allows participation in Interscholastic League activity during the senior year. Interscholastic League participation can be very stimulating and the honors and awards personally rewarding).

Vernon Regional Junior College (Vernon, TX) states that select high school seniors may be admitted to concurrent enrollment with permission from parents, high school principal and the Registrar of the College.

Austin Community College allows concurrent enrollment to high school seniors with authorization from a high school principal, with the stipulation that the course load can't exceed 6 courses including those at the high school.

Texas Women's University (Denton, TX) has a similar policy.

Angelo State University, in addition, allows high school students who have completed the junior year and are in the upper 10 percent of their class with an ACT score of 23 or more, to register for the full summer session for 6 to 7 semester hours per term, with credit given after high school graduation.

Southwest Texas State University (San Marcos) offers a program called Accelerated Achievers Admission Program (AAAP) in which you can as a high school junior begin to earn credit toward a degree during the summer session. For this program you will be required to be in a college preparatory program with a "B" or better average and have a composite score of 24 or more on ACT (or 110 on the PSAT) and a recommendation from your high school counselor or principal. Again, credit won't be given until high school graduation is verified. Or you can be admitted (with the same requirements as for AAAP) to SWT during the latter part of your senior year and take 6 semester hours of courses while completing high school.

Some of the larger school systems have developed programs for taking courses for college credit without leaving the high school campus.

The Houston Independent School District has a "College Study Option" developed for HISD by the Houston Community College System. Under this program HISD seniors may earn up to 18 semester hours of credit before high school graduation. Students don't need to leave the high school campus and can often even fit their studies in without extending the length of time they are in school during the day.

The options are many and the specifics may change, so you will want to explore what the colleges in your area offer. Consult the college's catalog, or talk to the Director of Admissions. If the school doesn't have a formalized program, they may make individual arrangements. Have documentation of your qualifications in hand and be prepared to wait in offices and/or come back several times to talk to the people who can help you.

CORRESPONDENCE COURSES

As a high school student you may enroll in college-level courses if you have the prior approval of appropriate school officials. Write for a catalog, "Independent Study by Correspondence", of the courses offered:

> Extension & Correspondence Studies
> The University of Texas at Austin
> Education Annex F-38
> Austin, TX 78712
> (512) 471-5616

Correspondence courses are a form of individualized instruction and the courses range from Psychological Foundations of Elementary Education (the first course in the required professional development sequence for approved programs in elementary education) to Engineering Drawing (an engineering graphics course in the department of mechanical engineering) to Greek, Latin, French, Italian, German, Philosophy, English Literature, College Algebra and Calculus.

A student must exert much self-discipline for this type of offering, but flexibility and individual attention offer some unique learning opportunities. Even though you may never see the instructor, you may develop a close relationship through letters, notes and other communications. You will need a good support system or a mentor at home or school to make this offering a successful one in most cases, and so we do not suggest it as the best option. However, if you live in an extremely rural or isolated area and can't find an option for working with peers, then this might be for you–tape recordings of your assignments and of the instructor's comments might personalize it even more.

EARLY ADMISSION TO COLLEGE

While high school/college concurrent enrollment is really an early admission to college, there are two routes which are more direct.

3-YEAR HIGH SCHOOL PROGRAM

You can graduate a year early from high school, if you have planned carefully. Make sure you have taken care of all of the state and local district requirements, such as History, Physical Education, etc. by scheduling required courses early in your high school years. Also plan for the advanced courses that will be useful or necessary for your college specialty area. You can double up on some offerings, such as taking two English courses in your junior year, but the Physics you want may require specific prior math courses, and language requirements for some colleges may have to be begun in your freshman year. Some of the more prestigious colleges still have foreign language requirements which will have to be met by high school credits or outside study and credit by exam.

EARLY ADMISSION

There is much variation between colleges and universities with regard to early admission. Skipping the senior or even junior year of high school again requires good planning, but may be best for you. Many high schools will even grant you a diploma *after* you have successfully completed your first year of college. Some of you who are extremely able may even be able to make the jump from eighth grade. Many students have made the accelerative leap very successfully, some earlier than others. If you have good mentors or advisors, strong family support, and good collegiate academic and personal guidance, this may be successful for you too. (e.g., Dr. Julian Stanley works very closely with the students who are admitted to Johns Hopkins University early, helping them to plan a course of action that will be right for their individual needs.) Again, staying with the educational preparation because it is exciting, challenging, and rewarding will certainly be better for you than becoming "turned off" to using your intellect and talents productively because of deadening, boring, and repetitive high school courses. This is a difficult decision, so get the best counseling you can locate–if possible, someone who is knowledgeable in the area of gifted education.

Some school policies include:

North Texas State University (Denton, TX) will consider your application on an individual basis; NTS requires you to be ranked in the top quarter of your class with a strong B average; have 3 units of English plus 2 units each of math, social science, and natural science or foreign language; have a combined SAT score of 1000 or ACT composite of 24; with letters from the principal or high school counselor and parents.

Texas Lutheran College (Seguin, TX) will grant you early admission after your junior year of high school if you are ranked in the top quarter of your class; have a composite SAT of 1200 or ACT composite of 30; with letters from the principal or high school counselor; and 15 units (3 English, 2 math, 2 foreign language, 2 social science, 2 lab science, and 4 electives).

Other schools may permit early admission on an individual application basis, while a few will state that they have *no* allowance for early admission. Inquire with the Director of Admissions or Registrar about the possibility if you feel strongly about early admission. A few colleges, such as the University of Chicago, Goucher College in Baltimore and The Johns Hopkins University don't require their applicants to be planning to obtain a high school diploma, simply requiring that the student be highly able and well prepared to do academic work. Thus if you are highly able but have not shown any ability to do academic work, you may not be considered. You should probably have a score of at least 1300 on the Verbal and Math portions of the SAT or 130 on the PSAT, 57 on SAT's Standard Written English Test (TSWE) and scores at the 75th percentile or higher on the College Board Achievement Tests for early admission. Some colleges in the nation may approach *you* if you have obtained high PSAT scores and have been recognized for other achievements. Look into their program carefully, looking for the guidance and personal attention to academic choices that were mentioned above, weighing it carefully against your other opportunities and options.

COLLEGE ACCELERATION

Acceleration after you are in college is much easier to bring about than in middle or high school. Advanced standing, summer courses, changing direction or shifting majors, graduate courses as an undergraduate have all become distinct possibilities.

Double majors permit you to follow two career lines simultaneously, thus keeping open later options for related careers. Usually the majors will have overlapping courses which can serve for the requirements in both fields. Planning is necessary, because some courses fit better than others. For example, if both electrical engineering and computer sciences require a physics course, the engineering physics may serve both fields, while the computer science physics may only suffice for that major.

Field and cooperative programs permit you to gain valuable practical experience along with your academic courses.

Double degree programs permit you to accumulate keys to more opportunity doors quicker. You may be able to earn a Bachelor of Engineering Science and Master of Science in Engineering by your choice of courses and sequences, or a BA and MA in Economics and Business Administration. Degrees in less closely related fields, but nevertheless fields dependent upon each other, such as law and engineering or foreign languages and agricultural economics give you tremendous flexibility, and individuals with such degrees are highly sought after for the combined specialization.

The crucial word in advice for acceleration seems to be

PLAN   PLAN   PLAN

with a bit of scheming and diplomacy and persistence on the side!

CHAPTER FOUR

What's Doing in Midtown, U.S.A.?

"What can I possibly find to do in this town?! All the really exciting activities are going on in places like Houston, Dallas, Fort Worth. Our school has some challenging courses and some fun things like German Club's trip to New Braunfels, or stage band performances, but I can't find anything else much worthwhile. There aren't any stage plays, no great museums, and jobs are the same old thing—fast food places and grocery carryouts."

If this sounds familiar to you, see if any of the following ideas might help get you out of the doldrums and into some more adventurous tracks. These are the kinds of things that are available in Bryan-College Station, one of the fastest growing cities in the nation, yet pretty characteristic of a mid-sized community in the kinds of opportunities it offers. Extrapolate to your own community and see what you can come up with.

MUSEUMS—NATURAL HISTORY, SCIENCE, ETC.
(Few museums are too small to at least consider the following!)

Classes to take:
Reptiles & Amphibians; Astronomy; Crypotography. If none are offered for your level or interests, the directors will usually be glad to put one together IF you ask, and then back up your request with some positive suggestions about what you'd like to have covered in the class and, perhaps, with names or signatures of at least a half dozen others who would take the class if an instructor can be found and the class is offered. You might even have an expert in mind whom you would like to have direct the class.

Classes to teach:
Offer to teach a course and back up your offer with some sign of expertise—a well-assembled collection, or recognition of your skill and responsibility from a teacher or respected adult.

One of the best ways of broadening and consolidating your own knowledge base is to teach others. You find the information in your repertory of knowledge that is fuzzy, then rework it and perfect it. Concepts take on added dimension when you have to search for the best way to explain them to others. By the time you've found 6 different ways to explain how star systems evolved or how amphibians hibernate and bears don't, your own understanding will have increased tenfold. Besides, you may find teaching is exhilarating, and a hidden talent!

Volunteer time:

Prepare exhibits and displays, gather specimens. Even in a small community there is opportunity for a museum to grow—perhaps your contribution will be the key. In volunteering, be willing to share the menial jobs the *director* has to do and then be alert to unique contributions *you* can make. Someone has to make all those tags to label the specimens; attending well to fine details, perhaps coming up with more efficient or creative ways to attract viewers to the specimens should lend credibility and trustability to your contribution. Next time you may be asked to *identify* the specimens *or* participate in the specimen *search*.

Jean Piaget started a star-studded career in epistemology and developmental psychology with just such an activity. At the age of 10 he published a short scientific article on an albino sparrow that he had discovered (the publishers were unaware of his age). About this time, he began helping the director of Neuchatel's Museum where he lived after school each day—he helped catalog the extensive personal collection of mollusc shells and began his own collection, which led to the writing of a series of papers on molluscs. Between the ages of 14 and 18 he published this series and attracted the attention of the director of the Geneva Museum of Natural History, who offered Piaget the curatorship of Geneva's prestigious Museum of Natural History (again unaware of his age). Piaget declined the curatorship to finish high school, but he was already on his way to a Bachelor's degree in biology by the time he was 18.

Join special interest groups:

Special interest groups can range from birdwatching and identification to rock hunting and/or gem-polishing, to researching historical landmarks and archaelogical hunts. Such groups, sometimes sponsored by the museum and sometimes spontaneously formed, are held together by the common interest and expertise of the members. There is a fine line for acceptance in such groups between sharing expertise and being "just a kid" who is tolerated because he or she is bright.

When Bill, who was interested in birds, joined an adult birdwatching group, he read avidly between field trips about birds they might see or had seen; he learned to recognize their calls as well as their body types and colors. When he identified by its flight pattern the next pied-billed grebe they spotted, he found that others began looking to him for difficult identifications. It was good being accepted as a fellow birdwatcher rather than as "a smart kid". Whether or not Bill becomes an ornithologist, he has acquired a wealth of general and specific knowledge about how one brings order to a segment of the world, and has developed a rewarding avocation in the company of other people who shared his special interest.

Sierra Clubs are another special interest group if you are interested in wild life, the out-of-doors, the environment and preserving the natural ecosystems of that environment. There are 12 regional groups, 53 state groups and many local groups. You can obtain information about this group by writing to:

> Executive Director
> Michael McCloskey
> 530 Bush Street
> San Francisco, CA 94108

If you are interested in stamp collecting, you might try to locate a local group with whom you can not only exchange stamps, but also share in the excitement of rare finds and completed series. Your community's college or university will be a good place to look for this kind of interest group. If there is no college in your community, ask your Postmaster if he knows about any such group in your town. He will usually remember individuals for whom he sets aside special issues, or to whom he regularly sells blocks of commemoratives. These groups usually meet to trade stamps, plan for meetings with other collecting groups in other cities, or to just talk about the general topic of philately.

MUSEUM, ART–OR COUNCILS FOR THE FINE ARTS

While mid-town size communities are not as likely to have an art museum, they will usually have a Council for the Fine Arts through which you may be able to find ways to participate in a number of the fine art areas. For the most part the same suggestions for participating apply as given for other types of museums. If no real museum exists, you can call your local Arts Council and get in touch with the director. Again, since she or he will usually be an overworked, underpaid individual, the first suggestions given to volunteers will probably involve making labels, collating materials, stuffing envelopes–helping with the things that must be done by the professional because paid staff are not available. If you can see your way through some of this without feeling that you have been taken advantage of, you may find opportunities for bigger and better things: meeting and talking informally with visiting artists, finding out about juried shows and the best ways to exhibit different types of art, recommendations to sought-after art teachers, shows in which to enter your own work.

Junior Docent or Curator Programs:
These programs are mini-courses in art history, since in order to skillfully guide others through an exhibit, a docent learns all about the individual works of art, the artists, their unique styles, interpretations of the works, etc. Through it all you can begin to develop your own evaluative thinking and determine implications for work you may want to pursue.

Performing Arts:
Through volunteer attachment with the Arts Council you may also become alerted to opportunities for performance in your own skill area. While you (or a musical group to which you belong) may not be invited to put on a full-fledged community concert, your offer to perform may be accepted for an intermission spot to accompany an art exhibit, or as an olio for a theater production. The opportunity to perform for a select public may be the needed exposure for other requests, which may lead to professional development or coveted provisions for learning or instruction.

A group of high school students who had been part

of a jazz ensemble in school, some of whom were interested in music as a professional career, approached the Lions Club and offered to put on the main concert for the community 4th of July celebration. They practiced long hours on their own, provided the committee with some good publicity material, and were the featured performers for the event. The core group of musicians received offers to perform at other places and times and all of the group gained much pleasure and experience, not only from the performance, but from the extensive and varied preparations that were necessary to put on the performance. The initial wedge was their "volunteering" to perform, backed by the excellent reputation of the school ensemble.

If your community doesn't have a local Arts Council:
    You can write to your state's Commission on the Arts and Humanities for information on possibilities for your participation in any general or specific fine arts activities in your area. The addresses for some of those state commissions are:

    Texas Commission on the Arts and Humanities
    P.O. Box 13406, Capitol Station
    Austin, TX 78711

(Or, you can call the toll free number, 1-800-252-9415, leaving a message asking them for any information on available opportunities in your area, and they will return your call or send the information.)

    The New Mexico Arts Commission
    Lew Wallace Building, State Capitol
    Santa Fe, NM 87501

    Oklahoma Arts & Humanities Council
    4400 North Lincoln Boulevard, Suite 258
    Oklahoma City, OK 73105

    Louisiana Council for Music & Performing Arts, Inc.
    International Building, Suite 804
    611 Gravier Street
    New Orleans, LA 70130

COMMUNITY EDUCATION

This type of education for pleasure is growing in most cities in an effort to make all kinds of educational experiences available to all ages of people in all walks of life, and in an effort to enhance the leisure time of people. Its outstanding characteristic of flexibility permits it to be very responsive to the wishes and needs of the community. You can find everything from advanced car mechanics to computer technology, from pottery making to foreign languages, and from aerobic dancing to Yoga meditation. Some of the types of offerings are listed below and you can make your own requests as well.

Health Classes:
Don't underestimate the exercise of health offerings. Chess players know the value of being highly fit–intense concentration and prolonged thinking seem to be much more readily available when an individual is in good physical condition. Some of the most outstanding intellects have been enthusiastic soccer or tennis players.

Avocations:
Taking time for enjoyable avocations and/or leisure can also greatly enhance your productivity. Some individuals engaged in intense intellectual endeavors, such as government, business management, physics, medicine, to name but a few, seem to profit from release of the mind through very opposite activities such as instrumental music or painting. Individuals who have decided to use their talents in the creative arts find that periodic explorations in other fields sharpens their creative abilities. Winston Churchill, in the midst of political or government crises, found respite and mental health in his painting.

Foreign Languages:
Facility in a foreign language is best assimilated in as immersive a situation as possible, that is, hearing and speaking the language. Community education classes may offer languages not offered in your school program, and, in addition, may provide group opportunities to help you expand your listening and speaking skills for a language in which you have already taken a basics course in school.

Professional Offerings:

In community education, courses are taught by individuals from the community who have shown expertise. Occasionally, a superstar professional may be persuaded to teach a course. A recent offering in Bryan/College Station was "Microcomputers, their use and programming" taught by a master and originator in the field. Those who had the necessary background for this level of instruction were able to take advantage of a unique learning experience.

Subsidiary Skills:

Tool skills, such as typing, which add to your flexibility in any type of work are typical offerings in a community education program. Depending upon your long term interests, an illustrative drawing or sketching class, the basics of flying airplanes, or a business management and planning class might add greatly to your repertory and prove invaluable in a later career. Be imaginative in your search as well as in your requests to your community education director. There may be realistic and practical limitations to offering the class you suggest, but if you use your interpersonal skills to persuade enough others to take such a class, it can usually be scheduled.

PRIVATE LESSONS

This is an option that probably goes without saying, and ranges from instrumental music to art to gymnastics. This option is a more costly one, but it is a most desirable and satisfying one for learning specialized skills. Sometimes your school teachers may be helpful in locating private instructors. You do want to locate ones who will help you proceed at your best pace and are experts in their field—incorrect technical skills can be very difficult to unlearn. If financing lessons is a problem that you or your family have difficulty managing, you might consider "bartering". Offering to help a music instructor with her group sessions, or cataloging instructional materials, or even mowing a lawn in return for lessons may sometimes be arranged. Instructors are often very agreeable to special considerations when their pupils have shown outstanding persistence in trying to develop their talent, as well as promise in the talent itself.

GROWTH AND SERVICE ORGANIZATIONS

Growth and Service Organizations (Scouting, 4-H, Church groups, etc.:

Membership in this type of organization provides a great opportunity to *explore your potential for leadership.* How you go about doing this is important, because obviously you don't just appear at a meeting and say "Hey guys and gals, I'm here to show you how to really make this group hum!" It's also obvious that each of us has a unique style of interacting that's best for us; you can find what yours is by being alert to the responses of others. How is your style being received? Are they ignoring your suggestions because you lack credibility? Research the facts for the next situation, have some examples ready of solutions such as yours that worked, and then learn to communicate your ideas parsimoniously (i.e., briefly) and lucidly (diagrams or charts are great depending on the project, how much time you have to prepare, and on whether your group would respond to this format). Are they ignoring your suggestions because you appear too domineering? Wait for the right opportunity to present and keep in mind that someone else may have some valid things to add to that great idea of yours, or even may have a *better idea* this time, and then accept the alternative with good humor. Others will consider your ideas much more valuable if you've sincerely considered their viewpoint and have respected their self-esteem. Be able to yield on small points in order to gain leeway on the big ones.

These organizations also provide marvelous opportunities to *practice communication skills,* an asset in any career field. The scientist may make great breakthroughs or discoveries, but if these can't be communicated to others in an understandable form the ideas are ignored or lost or subsumed by others. The physicist may be able to talk to other physicists in physicist's terminology, but must also be able to talk to scientists in other disciplines–the engineer, the biologist, psychologist–where jargon has no meaning, or has conflicting meanings; awareness of how to use analogies and models will help greatly to make ideas clear. Science of the future will more and more be accomplished by interdisciplinary teams–the medical researcher working on hypertension and blood circulation will team with the veterinarian who understands animal biology and the experimental animal, with the biochemist who can project life-chemical interactions, with the engineer who can design bionic systems to duplicate human tissue activity, with the statistician who can apply mathematical procedures and probability theory to data, and with the computer technologist who can build and program complicated instruments to monitor all that goes on and record and recall data as no human can. After all the technical requirements are fulfilled, individuals are needed who can communicate the results and the implications to the layman and the businessman who will be the audience and the mover for the implementation of these scientific discoveries. How successful a youth organization group is depends on how well its members communicate their needs, problems, and solutions.

Communication skills apply not only to scientists but also the artist. Those who are responsible for the education of architects and environmental designers have begun to realize that students who come to them with great talents and creative ideas for drawing and modeling and planning for space, but who don't know how to either put their ideas into the verbal medium on paper or orally are again limiting their chances for making those ideas live. Schools of architecture are beginning to demand that their students enter with verbal skills and be able to develop them as basic tools of the trade. Keep this in mind when your Scout or 4-H project requires a report, oral or written.

Learning *how to package ideas* so that they are attractive to others, catching people's attention, is another useful communication skill that can develop as you work and interact in growth and service organizations. Ideology and philosophies of living have to be packaged well in order to persuade others to partake of them. This same kind of eye-catching presentation can be used with academic ideas as well. In the field of gifted education, a man named Joseph Renzulli had some ideas for the way in which teachers could best plan the learning activities of gifted students in the classroom. While many words written about this plan of action told about the idea, it was a graphic trisected triangle with internal flow arrows that imprinted the substance of the plan in the minds of his audience, and Renzulli's Enrichment Triad Model took on lasting meaning for teachers (see what I mean about words? A graphic would have caught your eye *and* your attention and explained the example much more efficiently.) Logos, another packaging technique, have an additional effect of being easy to recall.

The specific *art of speechmaking* in communication skills can be another by-product of youth organizations. If you're really active in the group, there will probably be many opportunities to represent your organization at regional meetings, state councils, etc. One 1981 graduate of a local high school had served as representative to the Texas Council of 4-H from her district, and as such, met with about 30 other youth from all over the state to make decisions and plan for 4-H activities of the 160,000 other members. She was at ease (or conveyed "at ease") in talks to groups of people of all sizes and ages.

Expansion of knowledge base is an important activity of youth organizations, depending upon the quality of their membership and leadership, and may be a great chance for enrichment in a wide variety of topic areas. As the girl mentioned above says, "4-H is not just cooking and cows". A 4-H project done well and carried to the state or national level will have required many hours of information search and growth in knowledge about the topic area, in addition to the practical hands-on experience that is gained from such a project. Boy and Girl Scouting and Campfire Girls provide additional kinds of practical experiences, as members work on badges and ranks, again not just limited to camping and outdoor recreation. In Girl Scouting "WIDE WORLD OPPORTUNITIES" come to individuals who have gained expertise and shown leadership.

Finally, *interpersonal and social skills* can be practiced and perfected in these settings. Learning to relate to the needs of the others in the group in order to accomplish individual projects and mutual undertakings is a skill that will serve you well in your later endeavors. A group of high school students active in a local church youth group just completed another of their annual week-long treks to Appalachia to help people in need upgrade their homes and community. The trip and work and interactions with the Appalachians and each other required much of these kinds of interpersonal and social skills as they traveled and worked together. This is another aspect of leadership, one which may assist you in those professional interdisciplinary teams that were mentioned earlier.

EXTRACURRICULAR ACTIVITIES

Participate in your school's extracurricular life:
Conversation with high school seniors who were about to graduate and who were musing about the future scenarios which they had been assigned to write indicated that this kind of school-related activity had been very important in their lives. As they reflected on their individual experiences it became obvious to them that those who felt best about their high school experience were the ones who had been doing a variety of things and *cultivating a variety of friends.* They had seen the worth of others and participated in activities, developing their talents as a natural consequence of those activities. One of them who has had outstanding leadership experiences and a tremendous zest for life stated firmly, "Well, I've really enjoyed MY high school years. I've had many good friends that I did things with at school, but almost every weekend I would go to some 4-H or church youth meeting in another city where I'd meet new friends. Those people came to be good friends whom I'd look forward to seeing when I'd go to Waco or Temple or Tyler or wherever." We all could see that her enthusiasm was continually regenerated by the way she reached out to people and activities with them. In school, she had been a cheerleader, a drill team participant, a member of the band, but she had also been a serious contributor to her church and 4-H council, and a representative to a national leadership conference in Washington, D.C. The wealth of her experiences was not incidental, nor due to luck—she made everything she did yield positive results and she refused to let the undesirable "musts" get in the way of finding positive results.

One of the students found that some of his best experiences had come when he had been *acting independently*—a day at the state capitol on his own to testify or lobby for a bill which he felt was important, a cultural event in another state, editorials for the school newspaper (of which he was the editor) which didn't always meet the approval of administrators, newspaper lobbying for 'causes', an independent printing of his senior class's will which sold like wildfire. He never waited for activities to come to him, but made a point of jumping into those where he believed he could make the greatest impact.

Another student reflected that it wasn't until her third year that she had determined that she would *set aside* her *shyness and feelings of inadequacy* and become a participant. She joined track, became a member of a judicial Teen Court, entered art and poetry contests, and found many ways to explore just where her interest in people-needs and her skills and talents could best come together. These activities helped her to overcome some of her shyness and to have a positive enjoyable high school experience.

Extracurricular activities may *develop into your life's work.* Journalism, newscasting, and writing careers often have their beginnings on a school newspaper or yearbook staff. Musicians branch off into their own groups after experience with a jazz ensemble, or band experiences. Christopher Cross recently won many awards for his popular music and has become a seemingly overnite star; however, he had been playing in small groups long before that, played for fraternity groups in college, sold musical instruments during that time, and wrote music much of the time. Twelve year old Stephen Baccus from Miami, Florida, who will enter college before turning thirteen, has skipped grades, taken high school algebra at age 8, accumulated 23 college credits, programmed his home computer to sing songs, and passed a flying test for a pilot's license, plans to do his college work in Computer Science, television production and aviation. But these are sidelines to the show business career that he wants to pursue, an ambition which began with his part in an extracurricular activity, a south Florida production of "The King and I."

WORK EXPERIENCE

Gain a variety of work experiences:

If you're not yet old enough to be hired for a paying position, you may be able to lay the ground work for later opportunities. If your interest is in animals or medicine, you might offer to help a local veterinarian whom you know after school or on weekends. Helping to clean out cages may not sound tremendously attractive, but it does permit you to work with a variety of animals and observe procedures for animal care or even for surgery. By the time you qualify age-wise for paid work, that veterinarian will have been able to see that you are alert, willing and able; knowledgeable (if you've been reading everything you can find on the subject); and responsible (if he or she has been able to count on tasks well done by you). While students in colleges in many fields are now finding that cooperative programs give them valuable practical experience in between semesters of attending classes, if you've already had practical experiences while still in secondary school, you are already ahead of the game.

One high school student with a flare for business and highly into computers persuaded his father to underwrite an investment in an electronic game room, which, in addition to being an economically profitable recreational center, would also be a salesroom for computerized games; on the side, this student designed and programmed new games to be marketed. He decided to take a year after high school graduation to build the business foundation soundly; he now is attending Stanford while his microcomputer company continues with the assistance of six full-time employees.[7]

Working in a retail furniture store, or in a clothing merchandising position could be a dull, routine sales job OR it could be the opportunity to obtain some design experience, learn about how fashions are determined, manipulated, packaged, etc. One student found her fashion expertise, accounting background and public relations skills were the ticket to being asked to accompany the owner of the store on a buying trip to the wholesale centers in Dallas and Fort Worth. It would be wise to keep in mind when you seek out or accept paid work experiences that federal and state child labor provisions cover age requirements, work permits, hazardous occupations, student-learners, minimum wage requirements, moral and health standards, working conditions, and compulsory school attendance. There are also special provisions which cover the participation of minors in theatrical, television, motion picture productions, or any public shows. Union policies often affect not only "blue collar" workers but also practitioners in the fine arts area. It is not as important that you be aware of the exact

---

[7]Personal communication.

specifications (although knowledge of these may help you overcome hesitancy on the part of the prospective employer), but that you realize that the provisions exist to protect you from exploitation and lack of concern for your welfare. While some work experiences may be dead ends, you should be able to find those which will either give you practical experience for your future career goals or will give you contacts to help you in pursuit of that career.

Obviously, these aren't all of the resources a mid-size community offers for your educational enrichment. Check the resources of the metropolis (Chapter 5) and the rural areas (Chapter 6) also, the summer institutes and the independent pursuits. Then try some creative brainstorming to improve the list even further. You may be surprised at how productive such a session can be for you!

CHAPTER FIVE

Hidden Treasure in the Metropolis

Whatever opportunities are available to people in Midtown, U.S.A., are usually also there for people in the metropolis; it just seems harder to find them. It's like a Brugel or Hieronymous Bosch painting, with so much detail that it has to be shown in sections to see what's happening.

E. Paul Torrance has written an interesting article you may want to read entitled "How Gifted High School Students Can Continue Growing Intellectually" (published in *The Gifted Child Quarterly,* Vol. 12, 1968). His many suggestions include such things as associating with university research projects or working as an apprentice in theater and art productions, joining other gifted young people through the MENSA international organization for people with IQ's higher than 98 percent of the general population, and taking time out or a break from the usual path to do such things as develop an invention, write a stage play, or learn new art techniques with a master. Dr. Torrance is very much attuned to the needs of gifted youth and you might find his article helpful to your own thinking.

Since many of the ideas in Chapter 4 will be applicable for you, just a brief reference will be made to them here and elaboration given only for ideas more specific to the metropolis. One thing that needs to be emphasized is that when anyone suggests enrichment opportunities for you, there is a great difference between VIEWING and DOING. Since you're most likely to be the kind of person who is searching for "What can I do?", this is probably more of a problem for those who plan for you, than for you who plan for yourself. Some of the outlets suggested in this chapter may even include some great VIEWING opportunities. The opportunities may give you recreational and aesthetic pleasure, which are good in themselves–the artist, the musician, the craftsman, the writer can not do without the VIEWER. And a perspective of the accumulated wealth of mankind's knowledge and productivity can not be obtained without some VIEWING. But for your own development, take time to go beyond. "How does that relate to what I'd like to DO?" "Would I DO it differently?" "Can I FEEL the technique the artist, or the musician, or . . . used?" "Where and when can I TRY that technique?" You might call it ACTIVE VIEWING. Make sure your plans include DOING as well as VIEWING.

VIEWING RESOURCES

Museums, planetariums, arboretums, libraries:
These kind of resources of large cities provide outlets for almost every interest area imaginable. You can, at some time or other, browse through extensive special collections of everything from contemporary art to the Old Masters, topical literature about the Women's Movement to Black History, Calder mobiles to actual size oil well structures, the Wright Brother's plan to nuclear submarine models, African tapestries to Persian relics. Cost is usually nominal and you can focus intensely on some one interest area, or scan a whole world of interests. Many museums have classes for all levels and ages of participants, with extensive expertise available for instruction, ranging from specialized art techniques to how to classify archaeological collections. The availability of specialists in many fields for lectures and demonstrations lends special depth to the museums of the metropolis.

Opera performances and ballets, symphonies and brass ensembles, musicals and Shakespeare:
Free offerings in any of these categories may often be found in many metropolises. The city of Houston uses a large inner city park to provide such resources. Check publications such as the Texas Monthly or Texas Homes for the dates and locations of special performances. These particular publications also give information about performances in all the cities of Texas and in the artist-based small communities, such as the Shakespeare plays presented at Winedale by the University of Texas drama department or the James Dick music festivals at Round Top. Other areas of the country have similar publications. But, enough of the VIEWING, information about which you can also locate in your cities' newspapers, opportunities which can be obtained at a variety of costs from free to very expensive.

SPECIALIZED TALENTS

Learn an unusual skill:
How to fly a plane, construct three-dimensional kites, build transistorized models, read Aramaic, do American sign lan-

guage, or navigate by the stars are probably not skills that will be your usual entry criteria for most careers. But they do introduce you to the unusual, both in activities and people, and they reinforce creative approaches to life. Becoming accustomed to using your whole brain capacity instead of confining yourself to the left brain activity required by most academic endeavors appears to require a conscious attempt, even by gifted individuals.

We have only recently begun to realize that most of our academic endeavors have strongly developed only the left hemisphere of our brain, and that most individuals have not even begun to use their right hemisphere, a loss of potential ability. We now believe that each half of the brain processes information in a different way—the left hemisphere analyzes information in a verbal, sequential or step-by-step no-nonsense mode, while the right hemisphere "visualizes" information in a spatial, intuitive, holistic and nonverbal mode—and that the two modes can complement each other if we allow both the opportunity to function. A book by Betty Edwards, "Drawing on the Right Side of the Brain" (Boston, Houghton Mifflin Co., 1979), which you might enjoy reading, gives a good explanation of how to go about doing this. Despite the title, the book is not just for those who would like to draw, but for those who would like to learn to use both sides of their brain.

Private lessons:

For talents in music, art, and psychomotor skills, private lessons are most important. See Chapter 4 for ideas on this option.

APPRENTICESHIPS

Locate a professional:

Find someone in your interest area whose work you admire and ask whether you might serve as an apprentice. Architectural firms, interior decorators, florists, veterinarians, radio or TV station personnel, newspaper or magazine staffs might give you valuable experience (or help you decide which of your talents you would most enjoy developing and applying). The term "apprentice" will imply that you are a learner who is especially interested in the profession, that you aren't too proud to learn from the bottom up, and that opportunity to learn from an expert rather than money is the motivating force for you at the present time.

Make an appointment directly with the professional; if you don't seem to be getting a hearing for your request (receptionists tend to guard their employer's time carefully), patiently and persistently wait in person for an opportunity to talk. Come with credentials in hand, such as a letter of recommendation or a recognized award or achievement in this skill area; perhaps, a portfolio of relevant things you have done.

Newspaper and magazine staffs:

They may be willing to take on an aspiring journalist if you can convince them that your "help" will not interfere with their tight production schedule. This may require initial willingness to be a runner, file old news stories, do library research for a story, manually collate special material, or even stuff envelopes. Having a well written and researched, timely and exciting story available at some point may be a later entry to a more desired level of participation. Being alert to the techniques and procedures that the staff uses in their work will place you in position to fill in a needed gap, another possibility for upward movement.

Explore the possibilities of doing a similar stint with a textbook publisher or a public relations firm. Again, the approach of wanting to learn from an expert will be most likely to allow openings for a young, inexperienced student. There will be time after you've been personally accepted to show your special talents for the field.

COMMUNITY PROJECTS

In a large city, there are inevitably many community projects with which you could gain experience in public relations, management and planning or political action.

Service projects (for a common cause such as 'cystic fibrosis'), **civic proposals** (as for an inner city park or a center for senior citizens), and **political campaigns** welcome volunteer help. Examine with care; make sure the project is one you can morally and rationally support and that the kind of experience you can gain from it will be part of your growth as well as a service to the community.

If you are interested in political science, law, psychology, or other social sciences, the experience may serve later as addition to a resume, as well as giving you practical knowledge and experience now to understand theoretical material in later courses. Having been active in the lobbying process for legislation or in the politics of the city can give you far better insight than several classroom law or sociology courses.

CLUBS, SPECIAL INTEREST GROUPS

Join or organize a club:

Through teachers in your school, find out about other students interested in a special subject area, such as chemistry, history, English literature, harp music, medicine, oceanography, space science, astronomy, etc., and form a core group. Then join forces with students from other schools; the pooled effort can increase your club's resources for leadership, guest speakers, field experiences, demonstration of techniques or materials in the field, and access to new information. Invite an adult (teacher or professional group) to sponsor your group and share their expertise with you. A city bar association might be approached to sponsor a high school pre-law group; an architectural firm or interior decorating firm might be willing to serve as advisors for educational meetings or planned projects. A space science or historical group might seek assistance from a museum, or work out a cooperative plan of exchanging material and professional resources for manual help with exhibits or a restoration.

Access in the metropolis to art and natural science museums, medical centers, the Space Center, a presidential library, symphony organizations, or Arts and Crafts Guilds are all resources which can be utilized directly, or indirectly through the contacts that they provide. Use your imagination to generate mutual benefits for your interest club and professional resource groups, and then look for ways to bring about the exchange of these benefits.

Great Books Foundation Program:

The Junior Program is designed for elementary and high school students. The group may meet at a school as well as in homes, libraries, or other such locations. Anyone may purchase one set of the series, a list of which is prepared for each grade and for adults, but only certified discussion leaders who have successfully completed a Great Books Leader Training Course may lead the discussion groups. Ask your English teachers about the availability of such a group in your area. If you want more information about the program write to:

Great Books Foundation
307 N. Michigan Avenue
Chicago, Illinois 60601

Growth and Service Organizations:

Probably the most obvious and least expensive outlets in the metropolis for enrichment under an organizational umbrella are the youth organizations *such as Scouting, YMCA and YWCA,* and some church organizations. Although these structured programs sometimes suffer from lack of creative adult leadership, most often they do try to provide opportunities for interacting with youth from other areas, other cities and states, and even internationally. All the possibilities for *gaining leadership, communication,* and *social skills* that were described in Chapter 4 apply here as well. If the programs aren't challenging enough and you see no way to change that with the present peer group or leaders, do move on to other activities. Consider whether your special talents can be better developed in some other way.

Volunteer work:

Groups such as Candy Stripers or other medical service groups, Big Brother-Big Sister programs, Day Care Centers, and Geriatric Centers can put you in touch with the lives of many people different from yourself and contribute to your own sense of self-worth. Playing checkers or dominos with an octogenarian may not seem to take much intellectual prowess (on the other hand, it just might!); but the opportunity to get a sense of history from people who have lived through eras that you can only read about can not be equalled by any media. One high school senior who worked with a Geriatric Center developed a practical and much needed recreational program which could be carried out by the staff and "oldsters". Although she was interested in a social services career, others with talents for drama, music, or show business, could find real, appreciative audiences here.

EXTRACURRICULAR ACTIVITIES OF YOUR SCHOOL

Chapter 4 covers this subject extensively. Your schools may be so large and impersonal that you fail to see the trees for the forest. Extracurricular activities such as orchestra, band, chorus, yearbook staff, school newspaper staff, chess club, Spanish or German clubs, stage productions, and forensic activities may seem to be geared for a limited few students. This is no time for shyness or hesitancy even though the skills needed may only be a side talent that you want to explore or develop. The interaction with a variety of students with a variety of talents can broaden your experience base. These activities may serve to establish the additional Base Camps talked about in Chapter 1. They may also help you discover new talents or find new uses for the ones you already knew you had.

Don't forget about *University Interscholastic League* or any other competitions that bring you in touch with students from other schools. You may not always come home with laurels or trophies, but the wide friendships made are great. It's pretty neat and reassuring when you're spending your freshman year at a university far away from home to meet students you competed with back at your home base in Austin, Texas, or Kalamazoo, Michigan, or Portland, Oregon, or wherever.

Future Problem-Solving Bowls are becoming a more frequent offering in schools. This is another exciting opportunity to challenge your right and left brain to the limits, using your creativity as well as your academic knowledge. If your school doesn't already have such an offering, suggest it to your teachers and you might even assist in the organization of it. Write to Dr. Anne Crabbe[8] for information about this type of ac-

---

[8]Dr. Anne B. Crabbe, Future Problem Solving, c/o Coe College, Cedar Rapids, Iowa 52402.

tivity and how to get it organized so that your school can participate on a national basis.

SUMMER PROGRAMS

In many larger cities you will have access to many special summer programs. Some are well established (see Chapter 7) offered on a regional or national basis, but some may arise locally. Ask your counselors or principal or special topic teachers about such offerings. Some may be very academic, such as science or medical institutes, others may offer travel opportunities, such as three weeks in Mexico with a Spanish Club; or the combination of service with travel, such as a peace corps type program in the Dominican Republic. By the time such programs are publicized in the newspaper it may be too late to plan for participation. So check early and frequently with counselors, teachers, and school administrators.

Go back to your own Bosch-type metropolis now and examine it with a magnifying glass. See what else you might find that hasn't even been alluded to here. And remember, finding opportunities for enrichment in the metropolis is different than looking for choice merchandise in a department store; perhaps it is more like an antique auction—sometimes you have to creatively see the potential in an offering to select an item that is really extraordinary.

CHAPTER SIX

Where to Search in the Wide Open Prairies

"There's no one to talk to about what I'm most interested in—no one who knows enough about interstellar space—or the Inca civilization—or Beethoven's melodies in contemporary jazz—to challenge me to think through that mess of information I have."

"Most of the kids in school think I'm weird because I want to know more about set theory and—" "I'm afraid to let on that I know as much as I do about physics and that I really *like* reading Plato."

"I have to spend an awful lot of time just helping my Dad on the ranch," or "There's so much field work to do in the summer, I'd just never be able to go to any special institute."

"Out where I live there's miles and miles of nothing and no place to go" or "This town where I live is so small everyone knows everyone's past, present and future."

WHAT DO I DO ABOUT:

The aloneness of having no one to share my mind's best thoughts with?

The discouragement of being laughed at for thinking what I hope are intelligent thoughts?

The frustration of not having access to the worlds I know exist?

YOUTH ORGANIZATIONS

When you ask almost anyone what very able youth can do to develop their gifts and talents in a rural area, there is likely to be a long silence, and then "Well, I guess there's 4-H."

4-H is indeed a possibility, and we're finding out that it is an excellent one. Even people in mid-sized communities are realizing what a lot of opportunities 4-H offers for developing *leadership skills and communication expertise,* for *becoming* extremely *knowledgeable* about many topics ranging from the expected animal science and clothing construction to the less expected rocketry and photography, and *doing independent* *projects* in these areas, and for meeting and *associating with many exciting, capable youth from all over the state and nation.* But did you realize that animal science majors in college go on to develop food production plans in deserts and swamps for the underdeveloped nations in Africa, and that many fashion designers, textile experts, and decorators had their beginnings in basic clothing and craft knowledge? The opportunities for doing a project tailored to your exact interests, whether it be breeding of race horses or developing a minute motor for windmills or finding a cactus purple dye to imprint linen, are boundless; these are interests which will attract the advice and assistance of the best experts in the field, and then, with your development of them, may win national attention in 4-H competition. County Extension Agents are probably the most enthusiastic facilitators you will find anywhere. And best of all, their minds are attuned to helping youth work on these projects under the most isolated, difficult circumstances imaginable. You set the pace and the goals and they help you find the assistance you need and the audience for your final products. Read more about how these benefits can be realized in Chapter 4.

FFA and FHA are organizations in which similar opportunities are available. Leadership and communication skills can be important by-products of their meetings. Recently, at an annual FFA banquet on the Texas A&M campus, the main speaker of the evening was a young man finishing his senior year in high school who had been FFA state president for the past year. His presentation would have been a credit to some of the most highly known professionals; his speaking style, sense of humor and timing, and most importantly, the content and message were well planned and executed. Of course, he had had much practice, since, as an officer in the organization, he had been participating in and presiding over local and regional meetings throughout the state, for the past several years. This wasn't unusual–it's the usual procedure for active members who show leadership possibilities. It's a great forum for developing the skills that allow you to be competently front and center.

Summer camps, county and state fairs, and regional meetings also give you great opportunities to meet other very capable youth and the chance to meet someone who may even have some better ideas about your special area of interest or pet projects.

"But, what if I hate working with animals or have this consuming desire to write a great novel, dance in a ballet, explore life on the ocean floor, or my interest has nothing to do with the farm or the ranch?" Here are some other kinds of possibilities.

EXPERTISE AND INTERESTS

Become an expert at something:

The area of expertise doesn't necessarily have to be consistent with your career goal. Having a skill that is developed better than most people's and developed to the point where practicing it is no longer a drudgery but something you can't wait to do, is a fantastic source of re-Creation. That skill needn't be limited to musical instruments or athletic specialties. It could be juggling, magic (Johnny Carson started out with a repertoire of magic tricks), needlepoint, constructing violins, sandpainting, assembling and creating models. Such skills may provide bridges to other individuals with similar interests who can help open up a diversity of additional worlds to you. An outstanding photographic collection of desert flora and fauna, county fair scenes, or people at work, exhibited in a local bank, could introduce you to people who would like to own some of your works, or, even better would be able to arrange further outlets for your work and instruction for your talent.

Banks, museums, tourist centers, restaurants or perhaps even the county courthouse may be willing to display such artwork for a period of time. One young man persuaded a restaurant to allow him to display about 20 of his canvas paintings—some were purchased by patrons, but the major benefit was the exposure of his work and talent which led to other exhibits and the encouragement for him to continue painting.

Special collections:

Rocks, insects, plants, stamps, old books, etc. Not only does developing special collections become RE-CREATIVE but, also, the self-confidence gained from the expertise displayed in your collection, just as having an unusual skill, can transform all your other endeavors. It can help you accept your academic and creative gifts as something not weird, but 'different', not ludicrous, but 'something to be nurtured and used'. When you believe this strongly, others will too, and it won't really matter that some don't. One of the most difficult things in being gifted for you who live in small communities or schools is finding others with whom ideas can be shared seriously, others who can challenge and stimulate your mind and who can believe in your potential for going beyond the commonplace. So, activities which permit you to touch base with other out-of-the-ordinary persons have to be found; expertise at special skills, and knowledge through special collections are two ways of doing this.

Find external outlets for your productivity:

Send in your creative writing to journals and to publishers. By the time you have accumulated some rejections you may also have an acceptance. Discuss possible outlets with your English teacher or yearbook sponsor or your librarian. On one of your trips into a large city, stop by to talk to a reference librarian at a college or at one of the city libraries. She or he may even be willing to keep in touch with you to tell you of outlets of submitting your work which have come to their attention. Remember the example of Rachel Carson in Chapter 3? Her first story, published at age 10, was published in a children's magazine called "St. Nicholas".

Send a portfolio to the nearest county or regional newspaper of your short journalistic-style articles on some topic, such as historical figures from your locality, area political representatives, high school sports events, a background series on a local issue, recreational outlets within a hundred mile radius. Ask if they'd be interested in a similar series. A small town weekly newspaper may not be able to pay you, but the experience and exposure may lead to more profitable outlets. Regional newspapers often have sections devoted to various localities in order to entice subscribers in those areas, so you might use that idea in your persuasive letter.

Learn how to apply for patents, then *put together one of your inventions and patent it.* Even if it's not producible at the moment, you may find it surfacing later in your life. OR, you may even find a market for it now! The new invention might be anything from a fascinating board game that you have dreamed up to a specialized tool for repairing tractors.

Talent and achievement contests:

G. R., a high school senior, won a $1000 prize by writing an essay for *the Sons of the Republic of Texas* state contest. Each year an essay topic is selected which reflects student awareness of Texas history. The 1981 topic was "The Texas Navy, with emphasis on its role in winning and maintaining the Independence of Texas." Ask your social science or history teacher about this contest or similar ones in your own state. Another Texas high school student won a six week exchange trip to Germany, along with 39 other students from across the United States, by competing in an *essay contest sponsored by Volkswagon dealers.* Be on the lookout for such promotional contests; check their authenticity with your school officials; and work with your parents to make sure that the arrangements of such a trip would be carefully done with attention to the safety and welfare of the award-winning students.

The *National Historical Society* conducts an annual College Scholarship Essay Contest with awards going to high school seniors who are entering college in the fall of that year. Prizes are awarded for the best historical essays on any one of three topics, with the topics specified for each year. In 1980, the topics were Pancho Villa and the Mexican Border, Stephen Kearney and the Conquest of New Mexico, and The Pueblo Revolt of 1680, with awards of $1000, $500 and $300 in each category for first year college expenses. Check a current issue of American History Illustrated for details of this year's contest.

If your school is not large enough to sponsor a science fair, ask your science teacher for information about entering the nearest one. *Science Fair projects* have been the entry points to exciting possibilities for many youth. One student whose school did not conduct a Science Fair, worked closely with one of her teachers on a biology project which she had been generating for several years. She entered her project (with the teacher's assistance) in the Regional Fair. Her entry went on to the International Fair in Milwaukee, where, in competition with about 500 other entries, she won three awards—one from the

American Medical Association, to be a guest at their national meeting in Chicago; one was a trip to NASA as an honored guest to be present when the data came in from the second satellite to pass Saturn; and a third from NASA to take her teacher to California to observe the flyby of Saturn. The awards also involve money prizes and will undoubtedly result in her meeting with many knowledgeable and influential people in the field of medicine. This is a great beginning for the medical research career that she envisions! Addresses for information on Science Fairs can be found in Chapter 9. And don't forget to participate in as many as *your school's University Interscholastic League activities* as possible.

The opportunity to participate in forensic, music, math competitions, and the like with a larger student population gathered from all the different schools in Texas, challenges you to hone your skills, and allows you to meet other highly capable students who also have wide interests. Again, it's a process of broadening your view and opening up new possibilities for developing your own skills and talents, and is an especially important outlet for students from smaller schools and in rural areas.

PEOPLE AND MATERIAL RESOURCES

Get in touch with resources:

Contact libraries that specialize in lending books by mail, if you're too far away to make frequent trips. Texas is divided into a number of library regions, each of which provide somewhat different services; (other states have their own systems.) Some regions offer a *Books by Mail Public Service,* from which you can obtain a catalog of their holdings. The books are, for the most part paperback editions, but many classics and scientific texts have been printed in paperback. You then mail in a list of the books you want, they're sent to you just as in a regular lending service, and are due back at a certain date. Write or stop in to check with the reference librarian or director of the nearest public library to see whether your region has this service; you might even try several regions if the nearest can't help you.

You may be able to *locate a microfiche reader* to read material that is stored on microfiche–scientific journals, historical documents, and the like. Perhaps an arrangement can be worked out with a lending library, just as in the Books by Mail Service.

Subscribe to magazines or journals:

Keep in touch with the newest in the field. Science News is such a publication, published weekly as an 8-page newsletter, and containing articles on the very latest that is happening in a wide variety of scientific disciplines. The content ranges from the physical sciences (macroscopic laser quartum) to the biological (magnetism in algae) to the behavioral (depression after spinal injury). The articles are extremely well-written, technical but understandable, and of such depth that the publication is of interest even to the professional in the field. Write to:

> Science News
> Subscription Department
> 231 West Center Street
> Marion, Ohio 43302

There are many literary publications, as well as publications in other ares of study. Ask teachers for suggestions; they may have a copy or two to give you a better idea of the content and style and to see if the material interests you enough to make the subscription investment.

Communicate with others:

Obtain the names of students in foreign countries who want to be *Pen Pals* from your school's foreign language or English teachers. One individual who began, in fifth grade, a pen pal relationship with a person in England and kept with it faithfully, found an opportunity to travel to England as a sophomore in high school. She spent two weeks with the pen pal's family learning all about life there, and now, 10 years later, will be visiting with her again, this time in the U.S. You can also develop *your* foreign language skills rather than depending upon a pen pal to practice their English. You never know when you will be able to visit or travel in their country. While some pen pals may not continue to respond, or your interests may change over the years, it can be a good experience for many people.

HAM Radio could be a great way to be in contact with others who have similar interests. HAM radio enthusiasts are not confined to reporting emergencies, so search around for a HAM operator, learn how the system works, buy or construct your equipment, and enter a world of "voice" people.

Exchange with a city cousin:

You may think that no one else would care to be "stuck in your little town" or "out in this lonely place", but you may find that your cousin or friend would love to get out of the city for a few weeks, would even be willing to trade places and try your job or your living style. The chance to browse in art galleries, museums, the Space Center, or to tour legislative buildings, industrial plants, merchandising marts, may be as "old hat" to them as it would be a welcome change for you. And the exchange may give you a new perspective on a few of the advantages you may have become dulled to, such as the peace, beauty, and quiet in which to think. (Many people find that their most productive or creative thoughts come when they're doing repetitive manual labor—and if you have a notebook and pencil in your pocket to jot down ideas when you get to the end of the tractor row you may accumulate a gold mine of ideas for new projects, poetry, writings, music, or inventions, ideas just waiting for some later development).

Independent Study:

Correspondence courses have their advantages and disadvantages, but are a possibility that you might explore. See Chapter 3 on acceleration for information on this possibility. Foreign language tapes and records can improve your linguistic skills.

Offering to *research a product* for a company is another possibility. Be on the lookout for new products in magazines such as Newsweek, or Popular Mechanics, or home-oriented magazines. If the company is a fairly well established one you might scientifically "test" the use of the product, find some additional creative uses for it, and then write the company telling them generally what you have been doing. They may be interested enough to respond with requests for documentation (details, photographs, etc.), and hopefully some tradeoff value for you. Some companies are looking for product testers–be sure to check with knowledgeable disinterested parties first to determine the safety of the product and the legitimacy of the company before you "engage gears". Other ideas can be found in the separate chapter on independent pursuits (Chapter 8), along with ways to go about doing this. Independent studies is an opportunity for anyone anywhere if your learning style is compatible with working alone with a minimum of guidance and much self-direction.

Community Projects:

These projects can be a willing recipient for your enthusiasm and creative efforts, and a source of later helpful contacts as you pursue your education. If you live in a very small town, you or your family probably know about any and all community projects that are either underway or need doing. Give some thought to the project, accumulate all the background information you can, put this together with a few new creative suggestions for the project and an offer to see the ideas through with your own physical help (or the help of friends). Be prepared with diplomacy to overcome resistance from those who would do things "the same way we've always done it" and from those who feel strong "territorial" rights. Historical restorations are a possibility; sometimes the initial work (after the ideas) may have to be fund raising, but even there you may be able to use and develop your business management, creative problem solving, interpersonal communication skills, and leadership skills. The public relations needed may present opportunities to use journalistic or interviewing skills, artistic sign and poster designing, or even the assembling of a newsletter for potential patrons. The Harper Fredericksburg historical restorations in Fredericksburg, Texas, among many others, have had their beginnings in this way. The historical offshoots for your own interest could be tremendous.

Be a PEOPLE LISTENER and WATCHER:

There is a small rock shop in Llano, Texas. The owner has a

fascinating wealth of information about rocks in the area, the work of the mining engineering students who come there annually from nearby colleges, marble sculpture in Vermont, the kind of headstones famous people have in the cemeteries in New Hampshire. A hot afternoon spent talking with him could pass very quickly for a rock or sculpture buff. You can probably think of a dozen other possibilities of people who have time to spend with you because of age or disability, but who are fantastic *primary sources* for historical research. As a youth, you will tap a rich vein because such people are usually so pleased that you will listen that they will share perspective and information that can't be found in secondary reference sources.

(As an aside, for more specific information about where to find rocks in their natural geological settings, look for Chamber of Commerce brochures. For example, the Fredericksburg Chamber of Commerce and the Fredericksburg Rockhounds furnish a brochure which gives directions for tours which you can take through the gem and mineral trails of the Texas Hill Country. The Texas Parks and Wildlife publications also provide a wealth of information about a wide variety of natural and historic sites for exploration. Other communities and states have similar publications.)

Summer Stock:

Your community may occasionally have access to a summer stock stage production. Volunteer stage hands are always welcome, and you might even get a walk-on part. OR, you may convince a few friends to put together a production that will be welcome entertainment for a hot summer evening. A melodrama with popcorn, pop, and homemade ice cream could finance a more ambitious production during the schoolyear, or the whole town might turn out for a product that the community needs. If you all have "your act together" (pardon the pun)—the production rehearsed, logistics planned, publicity developed—and present the idea to the town elders or council *(you'll know* who runs the town) as a 4th of July celebration special (or for some day of unique historical significance for the town) you will be in business. More than one drama career has had its beginning in a small town production.

Get a home computer:

Computers will soon be as commonplace an item in the home as calculators now are (as you know, calculators once were huge, immobile and awkward but now are available in minute transistor form.) Home computers can now be obtained for the cost of a stereo, $700-$1000, or less if you have an old TV to hook into. For some of you this may be unrealistic, but for others, the investment will be possible. Once you have learned computer language and programming, you can do everything from playing games to running all of the machinery on the farm or in the household, to completing bureaucratic forms such as the income tax, to composing music, to writing, learning about, and solving complex scientific problems. Manuals are written that can get you started and keep you moving on to the most complex types of programming. Some of the computer production companies have sponsored newsletters which keep you informed on the latest uses and possibilities and about the people who are doing special projects with computers.

With these ideas, as a beginning, you can probably generate many more. So, don't reach adulthood saying "What could I do stuck out there in the boondocks?!" Instead, use the strengths of the small towns and wide open prairies to your best advantage.

CHAPTER SEVEN

Special Institutes and Summer Programs

Summertime offers a special sort of magic for school children and students, a magic that is forgotten by many people as they move on into their adult lives and careers. That magic stems from stepping out of the routine schedule that has guided activities from September to June, into a different pattern and pace. Granted, the pattern may sometimes be just as rigid and the pace as hectic as the school schedule was, but the shift can allow other skills and talents (areas of capability) to surface, and does put you in a position to assemble a perspective on what you've been doing and where you've been going throughout the rest of the year. Some careers also allow this kind of "sabbatical" or periodic "time out", but some people just allow this special time to dribble away without catching any new glimpses of themselves. Or they allow "busyness" to act like white noise, drowning out any inner messages or insight.

So when more "programs" or institutes or classes or jobs are suggested to fill those summer days, keep in mind that you need to decide which ones will fill your needs, whether those needs are trying out a new skill, developing an old one, challenging your intellectual limits, doing an independent study, earning funds for a future activity, or–yes!–just allowing yourself time to daydream, reflect, create a new idea, or think about your world and you.

There are so many summer programs available that it will be impossible to cite all of them. The suggestions offered here should give you an idea of the scope of programs and give you some initial leads to investigate. Don't be limited by the suggested ones however; as will be described in Chapter 9, there are avenues which *you* should pursue to find the best possibilities unique to your area and/or interests.

The Porter Sargent Publishers, Inc. assembles an annual listing of camps and programs throughout the nation, as well as a few international programs, *"Guide to Summer Camps and Summer Schools."* Their 21st edition was for 1979-80. The publishers invite any program to submit their description but the items are given a limited screening and checked for accuracy before being included.

The camps are indexed and listed by program emphasis and cross-indexed by geographic location. Information on appropriate age and sex of participants, number of participants per session, director's name and address, cost per session (although costs may have increased since publication of the Guide), dates of the sessions included, and a description of the type of content emphasized and the type of activities available. The content emphases range from the usual to the unusual, including chamber music, art in different forms, drama, ballet, languages, science, and outdoor survival. Examples of a few of the offerings included in this Guide are:

1) "Pre-College Foundation Program" at the Rhode Island School of Design for 15 to 17 year old students; $800 per 5-week session which is a pre-professional introduction to the visual arts in an industrial and academic setting.

2) *"Summer Music Experience"*, run *in conjunction with the Blossom Festival Season of the Cleveland Orchestra* (Ohio), for 14 to 17 year old students; $950 for a 6-week session which permits a variety of instrumental music experiences with the orchestra along with intensive private lessons.

3) *"Teton Science School"* for students from 10 years on up; $113 per week for sessions which use the Grand Teton National Park (Wyoming) as an outdoor classroom to study environmental awareness, ecological relationships, field biology, conservation and natural history; and

4) *"Spanish Workshops of Guanajirato"* sponsored by the St. Stephen's Episcopal School of Austin, Texas, for high school students who have had a minimum of one year of Spanish; $975 for a 6½-week session in which participants study the language, literature, culture, customs, and history of Mexico, while living in homes in Guanajirato, Mexico, and under the supervision of the Director, Dr. Phillip Hadley.

In addition, there are special camps for developing special skills such as gymnastics, horse care and riding, tennis, choral music, crafts, etc.

For an afternoon of fascinating browsing at your local library, this directory is recommended; if not available there, write to Porter Sargent Publishers, Inc., 11 Beacon Street, Boston, MA 02108.

Of special interest are some national programs which have been operating consistently for a number of years. They are:

1) *Pre-College Summer Programs offered by Carnegie-Mellon University;* six-week programs for high school students who would like to explore their aptitudes and interest in the fields of architecture, art, design, drama or music. Information may be obtained from:

> Carnegie-Mellon University
> Pre-College Summer Programs
> Warner Hall
> 5000 Forbes Avenue
> Pittsburgh, Pennsylvania 15213

2) *Career Discovery Program at Harvard,* which offers a six-week career exploration in architecture, city and regional planning, or landscape architecture to high school students, college students, and adults. Practical knowledge is obtained through field trips, discussion, workshops and lectures. The address is:

> Career Discovery Program
> 504 Gund Hall
> 48 Quincy Street
> Graduate School of Design
> Harvard University
> Cambridge, Massachusetts 02138

While the particular programs described above undoubtedly require above average ability in particular talent areas, some programs have been especially developed by professional educators of the gifted to better meet unique needs of gifted students. Duke University has published a listing of a large number of programs in "1982 Educational Opportunity Guide. A Survey of Educational Programs for the Gifted." This survey lists the educational programs in the 16 southern and lower midwestern states in which Duke University conducts annual talent searches for mathematically and verbally precocious students as part of its Talent Identification Program (TIP). The programs that were surveyed are those designed for students from grades 7 through 12; they include Saturday programs and seminars, as well as a great variety of summer programs. The Guide also lists a few selected high quality programs outside of the TIP area, and then describes in detail Duke's summer residential program for bright students. This latter program offers courses in American History, French, Latin, Mathematics, and Writing; it is intended primarily for the participants in Duke's annual talent search (TIP), although applications will also be considered from students outside the TIP region. As a participant in the talent search you will have received a copy of the Guide; others may obtain a copy at a cost of $3.00 by writing to the TIP office:

>Talent Identification Program
>Duke University
>Durham, North Carolina 27708

Texas A&M University, through the Gifted & Talented Institute, offers an especially intriguing collection of topical areas for you to experience in their summer program. Currently, their programs are held on the campus of Texas A&M University at Galveston. They focus on such topics as architecture, marine biology, micro-computers, space science and veterinary medicine. Galveston Island provides a rich setting for each of the above topics. Their brochure describes this "Galveston Island Adventure" as an exploring and doing kind of program in which "numerous field trips and lab activities complement classroom instruction." Application for participation in this program requires current enrollment in a school program for gifted and talented youth, standardized achievement test scores at the 90th percentile or above, or demonstration of outstanding potential for academic and/or creative endeavor. Information about these programs can be obtained by writing to:

>Dr. William R. Nash
>Director, Gifted & Talented Institute
>Department of Educational Psychology
>Texas A&M University
>College Station, Texas 77843

The Gifted Students Institute for Research and Develop-ment, based at Arlington, Texas in cooperation with colleges and universities presents a number of different programs, some geared especially for grades 5 to 9, some for grades 7 to 12, oriented to exploration of computer programming, environ-mental issues, creative writing and journalism, theater arts, aquatic research, and similar topics. These programs are gen-erally two weeks in length and take place on the campuses of various Texas universities, as well as at Ann Arbor, Michigan, and Stevens Point and Green Bay, Wisconsin. The Institute also sponsors programs in other countries. Students must submit a recommendation from his or her school as to gifted qualifica-tion, and a limited number of scholarships are available for the programs. Additional details about any of these programs may be obtained from:

> Laura Allard
> Associate Director
> Gifted Students Institute
> 611 Ryan Plaza Drive, Suite 1119
> Arlington, Texas 76011

Programs offered by universities or public educational in-stitutions are continually being developed, so you will have to contact schools or be alert to references in news sources in order to locate them. One such example in Texas is the East Texas State University offering at Commerce, Texas. A week-long High School Academic Enrichment Program–Summer Camp for 10th or 11th grade students–is sponsored during which students work with college professors to pursue a vari-ety of academic topics which aren't in the usual high school curriculum. Participants for the Summer Camp are nominated by their principal or counselor as accelerated learners, and the cost is nominal. Since cost may well be an important consider-ation for you, it will be wise to look for such options in your area. The opportunity to spend some time with other students who have similar academic interest and ability in a vacation-like environment may be the stimulus you need for finding the best way to use your special talents. Additional information about the camp may be obtained by contacting:

>Joyce E. Miller
>Director,
>High School Academic Enrichment Program
>East Texas State University
>Commerce, Texas 75428

Additionally, the National Science Foundation has provided grants for programs at the state level. In Texas, four universities were able to offer Science and Mathematics Training Programs for High Ability High School Students during the summer of 1980. Continuance of these programs will be very much dependent upon governmental funding, but it would do well to be aware of the possibilities. These particular programs were situated at Harden-Simmons University at Abilene, Sam Houston State University and the University of Texas at San Antonio. A junior high school program was also offered at Sam Houston State University at Huntsville. Similar programs were offered throughout the country and you can obtain information about these from your counselor, or write to:

>Ms. Mary M. Rohlerman
>Project Manager,
>Student Science Training Program
>National Science Foundation
>Washington, D.C. 20550

Since participation in these programs is limited and highly competitive, and nominations are submitted only by principals, counselors or teachers, you need to obtain information through your school (see Chapter 9).

Medical centers involved in extensive research in the field often have programs in which very able high school students can become involved. The University of Texas System Career Center, M.D. Biomedical Sciences, offers an 8-week summer program, limited to 20 high school graduates. The participants work at a special project with a research scientist. Since nominations for this program arise from within the medical field, experience at a hospital or with a local medical center may be helpful; one of the 1981 participants had been active as a student-aide in her local hospital through the Medical Explorer Scout program. Check out the possibilities at special medical centers in your part of the country!

Music camps, band, orchestra and choral, and theater and speech camps are numerous throughout most states. Have your music director recommend one at the right degree of difficulty for you. A few require having attained some competitive awards during the year. The two to four week experience of private instruction and group rehearsals are the proving ground for many aspiring musicians, are a lot of fun, and a great way to improve your skill for the regular year's participation and competition.

Citizenship and governmental participation are the focus of Boys State and Girls State camps and again are attended by invitation through nomination.

If you haven't been able to locate what you need, for the price you can afford, at the location convenient for you, through the suggestions above, or through suggestions from your teachers and principal, try contacting a Regional Education Service Center for your area (20 of them in the state of Texas). Your school officials can give you addresses where such facilities exist.

And then, maybe, just maybe, you might consider giving yourself time to dream a little in between busy school years! It's OK too, you know!

CHAPTER EIGHT

Independent Pursuits

Just a few words about independent projects, an opportunity that school programs are beginning to recognize as particularly appropriate for gifted students. However, you probably know that independent projects have been around much longer than school programs have, especially if you've been having to act independently throughout your school years. After all, most inventions and discoveries have occurred when individuals attempted to pursue their own creative ideas or solutions to problems.

Independent projects can be very exciting because they are ones in which you can take an idea that is especially of interest to YOU, develop it with skills which are especially YOURS (not necessarily always school-related skills), and do it in a time frame that is designed to fit YOUR NEEDS AND PACE, to result in a product that YOU EVALUATE as pleasing or profitable. The gameroom business venture described in Chapter 4 under 'work experiences' began as an independent pursuit. The Science Fair project described in Chapter 6 under 'enter talent and achievement contests' was advanced and perfected as an independent pursuit since the student couldn't find a science teacher or course to support the study. Writing a novel or composing music are usually independent pursuits; a seventh grader with many interests is spending her summer "building" such a novel.

But if you're having difficulty getting something underway and yet you'd like to try an independent project, the following suggestions for proceeding may be helpful. They've been developed by Cynthia Roeder from a basic idea presented in a DOK publication[9] and she will be glad to suggest ways to implement steps. You can reach her at this address:

> G/T Resource Coordinator K-4
> College Station Independent School District
> 100 Anderson
> College Station, Texas 77840

P — Pick your topic. Prepare questions. Acquire a historical background on the topic to find out how people do what-

---

[9]Patricia Weber, PROMOTE, D.O.K. Publishers, Inc., 71 Radcliffe Rd., Buffalo, NY 14214.

ever they do in that field. Obtain lists of societies, museums, people in the field. Interview people to find out what hasn't been done in the field. Explore the future for this particular topic and what innovative development could expand that future. Jacob Getzels, a well known creative problem solver, emphasizes that asking the right question is halfway to the solution for any problem. So take time to generate many questions and then make sure you focus on the one(s) that really reflect the problem!

R – *Read. Research. Record references.* Gather information from as many different sources as possible, such as writing a letter to an expert, having a personal or telephone interview, using the library resource of books, newspapers, professional journals and government bulletins. Look for television specials on your topic. Talk to primary sources (such as the rock enthusiast mentioned in Chapter 4). After reading widely prepare a list of questions. Set up some guidelines for the kind of information needed and what kind of questions need to be asked. Research those questions; gather information or data. Ask someone to be your mentor. Enlist your mentor's aid to suggest key people and to arrange introductions with those key people; "Dr. So & So suggested that I come talk with you about a project I'm doing."

O – *Organize your information.* Use cards, notebooks, files, boxes, or whatever to put the information into accessible holding spots. Assemble your findings in a professional manner; observe the way that findings are organized in professional journals in the field. If collecting data, be as precise as the data requires, but not compulsive; weighing elephants to the nearest milligram doesn't usually make much sense. Prepare graphics if needed with careful attention to details. While Einstein might be able to scribble important formulas on a scrap of paper, your torn looseleaf paper with wavy lines may not inspire much confidence in the credibility of your findings, or the desirability of your design.

D – *Design your product or project.* Again take time to brainstorm for the most creative way to carry out the project. (Consider doing this with a few friends for some really expansive ideas.) After you have many ideas, evaluate them according to criteria that fit your needs (money needed, time required, interest to you, danger involved, available resources, etc.). Then focus on one and plan your steps carefully. Again, enlist your mentor's aid in suggesting an audience for your project.

U – *Use your product or project* to teach others about your topic. Chapter 4 under "classes to teach for museums" describes why this is valuable. You may find ways to alter your product in order to communicate it better. Advertise country-wide in a scientific journal for others who are interested in the project or who might like to collaborate with you. You might find a sponsor or perhaps even write a grant to support further development of your project.

C – *Challenge others to ask questions about your topic.* This goes back to U and the evaluations and alterations.

E – *Evaluate your project and Enjoy it.*

CHAPTER NINE

Of Cabbages and Kings

This guide has proposed many possibilities for both acceleration and enrichment, and given you some reasons for choosing to do one or the other, or really some of both.

Before you began to read this book, you may have believed that school programs and educational institutions were not available to help you develop your gifts and talents, or perhaps that it's all up to you. Not quite so. School programs, however, are guided by financial considerations, by the necessity to provide educational services for individuals whose abilities range from almost none to those who have almost unlimited abilities, and by the functional considerations of operating within structured guidelines. Your needs and your possibilities go beyond those structures. To search for ways that you can *add,* then, to what school programs can and do provide can then be taken as an exciting challenge. The community and its resources are there to be tapped by creative individuals such as you who can act independently.

The guide is meant to serve if you are a younger gifted student in junior high as well as if you are a senior high school student. The suggestions have been made general enough to be taken and applied at whatever level you need. Classes at natural history museums may most often be geared to younger students, but the options and facilities which are available could be altered to fit many ages and levels of ability if the demand exists, that is if you ask. The enormous growth of community education offerings reflects how responsive these resources can be to the needs of those who ask.

ATTAINING VISIBILITY

And, speaking of "asking," announcements about special programs, summer institutes, available awards, scholarship opportunities, science or other talent searches and the like come to the desk of all principals of schools and/or to counselors throughout the school year. Sometimes the information may be posted on appropriate bulletin boards and sometimes it is funneled to teachers of appropriate subjects, who then pass on the information to the students who they think will be most interested. But sometimes the information just gathers dust.

It may be up to you to inform teachers that you are interested and available for programs, especially for those which
occur out of the school year. The information is available, and it
is important that you indicate your interest so that you can be
considered or can participate. Grapevine information from
other students is not always reliable and will often come too
late for you to do anything with it. Get to know your principal,
even though in larger schools it may be tempting to simply re-
main anonymous. Respect your principal's busy schedule and
limited time, but be persistent and then follow through on information you do receive. If you've been active in the extracurricular life of your school your visibility may already be great
and you may often be considered. However, a considerate in-
troduction of yourself and your needs to a principal, counselor,
or teacher can add much in bringing your needs and interest to
their attention.

TASK COMMITMENT

Being persistent and thorough about seeking information
is one way of being committed to the task of developing your
talents and abilities through as many school and community
resources as are available and appropriate. There are some
other characteristics that will be sought in considering you for
the special programs and awards.

A high school counselor, asked about how he determined
which students to nominate for programs offered by the National Science Foundation, private foundations, or professional
institutions, responded that academic record was one of the
top indicators. In other words, unless a student has shown con-
siderable promise in past school achievement, a nominee will
"not even make the first cut" for these programs. This may be
discouraging for you if your efforts have not been in that direction. You will have to look for other resources, realizing that
some programs may require more academic persistence than
is compatible with your most effective learning style. A creative
search for more relevant offerings for you will be more productive than a defensive self-defeating struggle.

Look for opportunities which emphasize or make best use
of your talents in creative and independent efforts. For these

opportunities, recommendation or references may come from people who have observed your ability in settings other than at school, or who have worked with you at your best. These references are important because the most frequent concern expressed by community professionals and businesses about working seriously with youth, even gifted youth, is that they may be irresponsible, that they may not carry projects to completion, or not be reliable in keeping appointments and meeting necessary deadlines. Their concerns are real because they have observed that time commitments and schedules may not always *seem to* matter to some students. In reality, family, school, and peer social demands (whoever has power to penalize or withhold your privileges and sources of pleasure) tend to preempt your time schedule, as for example, when a term paper, a prom, or a family requirement loom. A letter of reference from someone who has observed that you are responsible in the *long* term, and that you can be counted on whenever *you* have control of your time will help put such concerns to rest.

TALENT AND SCHOLARSHIP SEARCHES

Some college admissions and many scholarship awards are based on recognitions for outstanding achievements. Entering achievement and talent contests was discussed in Chapter 6, but some additional information may be helpful.

The International Science and Engineering Fair is a source of awards and recognition, as well as an educational experience, and is one of the few competitions where the judges outnumber the contestants. The judges are scientists, engineers, doctors, and mathematicians and awards are granted in two groups: the General Motors ISEF Grand Awards and the Special Awards in a variety of disciplines. The Fair which took place in 1981 in Milwaukee, and in 1982 in Houston, will take place in Albuquerque, New Mexico, May 8-14, 1983. If your science teacher doesn't have the information or you don't have a science fair director, write for details to:

Science Service
1719 N. Street, N.W.
Washington, D.C. 20036

A nominal fee is charged for the rules booklet and for a listing of titles of projects performed and shown at science fairs.

Another outstanding scholarship and award competition in the area of science and mathematics is the WESTINGHOUSE Science Talent Search. The entry is a project report of about 1,000 words based on an independent research project in the physical sciences, engineering, mathematics, biological sciences, or behavioral sciences, along with a Personal Data Blank and national test scores and high school transcript. Annually, 40 winners are awarded an all-expense trip to a five-day Science Talent Institute in Washington, D.C. to compete for the final awards–ten scholarships ranging from $5,000 to $12,000 and 30 $500 awards. The benefit also includes admission eligibility for the most prestigious schools in the field and the recognition by top professionals. For more information, have your teacher write to the Science Service address given above since students must compete through their school's auspices.

The mountains are here to be climbed, and YOU CAN PLAN THE EXPEDITION! Where and how are the exciting elements that only YOU can supply. You have the best of equipment and the encouragement of educators and professionals everywhere.

BON VOYAGE!!